The Arduino Controlled by eForth

Chen-Hanson Ting

Offete Enterprises

The current Forth Bookshelf can be found at
https://www.amazon.co.uk/Juergen-Pintaske/e/B00N8HVEZM
All are available as eBook – the ones with P after the number as well as print book.

1 **Charles Moore** - Forth - The Early Years: Background information about the beginnings of this Computer Language
2P **Charles Moore** - Programming A Problem Oriented Language: Forth - how the internals work
3 **Leo Brodie** - Starting Forth -The Classic
4P **Leo Wong – Juergen Pintaske – Stephen Pelc** FORTH LITE TUTORIAL: Code tested with free MPE VFX Forth, SwiftForth and Gforth or else
5P **Juergen Pintaske – A START WITH FORTH** - Bits to Bites Collection – 12 Words to start, then 35 Words, Javascript Forth on the Web, more
6P **Stephen Pelc** - Programming Forth: Version July 2016
7P **Brad Rodriguez** - Moving Forth / TTL CPU / B.Y.O. Assembler
8 **Tim Hentlass** - Real Time Forth

9P **Chen-Hanson Ting** - Footsteps In An Empty Valley issue 3
10P **Chen-Hanson Ting** - Zen and the Forth Language: EFORTH for the MSP430G2552 from Texas Instruments
11 **Chen-Hanson Ting** - eForth and Zen - 3rd Edition 2017: with 32-bit 86eForth v5.2 for Visual Studio 2015
12P **Chen-Hanson Ting** - eForth Overview
13 **Chen-Hanson Ting** - FIG-Forth Manual Document /Test in 1802 IP
14 **Chen-Hanson Ting** - EP32 RISC Processor IP: Description and Implementation into FPGA – ASIC tested by NASA
15 **Chen-Hanson Ting** – Irriducible Complexity
16P **Chen-Hanson Ting** - Arduino controlled by eForth

17 **Burkhard Kainka** - Learning Programming with MyCo: Learning Programming easily - independent of a PC (Forth code to follow soon)
18 **Burkhard Kainka** - BBC Micro:bit: Tests Tricks Secrets Code, Additional MicroBit information when running the Mecrisp Package
19 **Burkhard Kainka – Thomas Baum** – Web Programming ATYTINY13
20P **Georg Heinrichs** – The ATTINY Project – Why Forth ?

August 2018 v6_2018_10_27

Contents

Tao of Arduino

Chapter 1. eForth for Arduino

1.1 Arduino as a Firmware Development Platform

All these years, I have been looking for microcontroller platforms on which I can teach people how to program in the FORTH language. I designed a training course I called Firmware Engineering Workshop. I could train an open minded engineer to program in FORTH in about a week, with a reasonable capable platform, i.e., a microcontroller evaluation board with a FORTH operating system loaded. Good platforms are expansive, and low-cost platforms are inadequate. What I did was to grab any microcontroller board at hand and used it. It did not work well because what I taught could not be easily replicated by people at home. People got frustrated when they could not reproduce results I demonstrated. Then, I found the Arduino Uno Board.

The microcontroller evaluation board I need must have a microcontroller with reasonable capabilities. An 8-bit microcontroller with a fast clock is adequate. 16-bit of 32-bit microcontrollers are of course much better. The board must have at least 8 KB of ROM memory and 1 KB of RAM memory. It must also have a USART port to communicate with a terminal emulator on a host PC. Any other I/O devices will be icings on the cake. The more the better.

Arduino Uno has all of the components I listed above. It is also inexpensive, costing only $29. It uses ATmega328P, a very interesting microcontroller which has 32 KB of flash memory, enough to host a FORTH operating system, 2 KB of RAM and many I/O devices to build substantial applications. Arduino Uno also has a USB port which connects to a PC and an USART device in ATmega328P. This serial interface is necessary for a FORTH system so that you can run and program ATmega328P interactively from a terminal emulator on the PC – as the complete Forth is on the chip.

Arduino Uno is a lovely machine. You connect it through a USB cable to your PC, and you can program it to do many interesting things. Its microcontroller ATmega328P, running at 16 MHz, is very capable of running many interesting applications.

The template of a sketch, which is the software in Arduino 0022, captures the essence of firmware programming in casting user applications in two statements: setup() and loop(). It eliminates all the syntactic statements required by a normal C program and exposes to you only the core of an application.

However, Arduino software insulates you from the intricate nature of ATmega328P microcontroller, its instruction set, and its I/O devices. Instead, you are given a library of useful routines which are used to build applications. The insulation initially helps you to program the microcontroller in a C-like high level programming language. However, being an 8 bit microcontroller, ATmega328P in C language will run out of gas when application demands performance. At this point, you will have to get down to the bare metal to push ATmega328P to its limit. Then, you have to learn its instruction set and all its I/O devices, and perhaps program it in assembly language.

The best alternative approach is to program ATmega328P in the FORTH language. FORTH exposes ATmega328P to you. You can interactively examine its RAM memory, its flash memory, and all the I/O devices surrounding the CPU. You can incrementally add small pieces of code, and test them exhaustively. An interactive programming and debugging environment greatly accelerates program development, and ensures the quality of the program.

Since 1990, I have been promoting a simple FORTH language model called eForth. This model consists of a kernel of 30 primitive FORTH commands which have to be implemented in machine instructions of a host microcontroller, and 190 compound FORTH commands constructed from the primitive commands and other compound commands. By isolating machine dependent commands from machine independent commands, the eForth model can be easily ported to many different microcontrollers. This model is ported to ATmega328P, and the result is the 328eForth system, which runs very nicely on Arduino Uno Board.

328eForth is optimized for performance. The number of primitive commands is increased to 68. Commands which are used to build the operating system but rarely used by you are hidden so that you are not overwhelmed with unused commands. Only 151 commands are exposed to you. The source code is written in AVR assembly. The code is provided so that you can modify it to suite your application. The entire system takes up only 5,156 bytes of the flash memory. leaving lots of room for your application.

Unfortunately, 328eForth can not co-exit with Arduino 0022. The hardware reason is that 328eForth allows you to add new FORTH commands in the application flash memory section in ATmega328P, and the commands which write application section must reside in the bootloader flash memory section in ATmega328P. 328eForth must occupy the bootloader section. We must over-write the Arduino program loader in the bootloader section. The software reason is that 328eForth is an independent programming language and operating system, and it cannot call library routines in the library of Arduino 0022.

If 328eForth cannot co-exit with the Arduino0022, why does anybody want to use it on Arduino Uno?

The best answer I can give you is that 328eForth opens up ATmega328P so you can see what is going on inside ATmega328P, and that you can program and debug it incrementally, and interactively.

The best example is blinking the on-board LED connected to D13 digital IO line. This is what the BLINK.pde demonstration program in Arduino 0022 does. When 328eForth is up and running, type the following FORTH commands to turn the D13 LED on and off:

```
20  24  C!   \ make D13 an output pin
20  25  C!   \ turn D13 LED on
0   25  C!   \ turn D13 LED off
```

You will find the complete explanation on the above commands in Section 9.2.

Needless to say, the heart of an Arduino Board is the ATmega328P microcontroller. If you like to fully understand Arduino and make the best use of it, eventually you have to deal with ATmega328P directly. You will have to come back and read the AVR Data Book of Atmega328P, DOC8271.pdf, from Atmel Corp on "8-bit AVR Microcontroller with 4/8/16/ Bytes In-Programmable Flash", which is a huge 566 page document. It is a dry technical document, not for casual reading. Actually, it is not that bad. Only when you have to drive one of the devices, like the I/O devices, the lock bits, the fuse bytes, etc., in ATmega328P , you open the respective chapter and learn all about this device, line by line, work by word. If you have 328eForth running, you can examine the associated registers, and all the bits in these registers will gradually make sense. Change these bits interactively, and observe the effects. There is no better way to learn these devices, and to make them work the way you want them to work. And, 328eForth is your best friend to do that.

1.2 What is FORTH?

FORTH was invented by Chuck Moore in the 1960s as a programming language. Chuck was not impressed by programming languages, operating systems, and computer hardware of that time. He sought the simplest and most efficient way to control his computers. He used FORTH to program every computer in his sight. And then, he found that he could design better computers, because FORTH is much more than just a programming language; it is an excellent computer architecture.

So what is FORTH really?

Many books and many papers had been written about FORTH. However, FORTH is still elusive because it has many features and characteristics which are difficult to describe. Now that it has moved from software to hardware, with technologies like FPGA and custom IC, it is even more difficult to accurately put it into words. Here I will try to look at it from a completely different angle.

FORTH is a list processor. It is very similar to LISP in spirit, but totally different in form. Both languages assume that all computable problems can be expressed and solved in nested lists.

FORTH has a set of commands, and an interpreter to process lists of commands.

FORTH commands are records stored in a memory area called a dictionary.

A record of a FORTH command has three fields: a link field linking commands to form a searchable list, a name field containing the name of this command as an ASCII string which can be searched, and a code field containing executable code and data to perform a specific function for this command. It may have an optional parameter field, which contains additional data needed by this command. The link field and name field allow the interpreter to look up a command in the dictionary, and the code field provides executable code to perform the function assigned to this command.

A FORTH command has two representations: an external representation in the form of a text string with ASCII characters; and an internal representation in the form of a token, which invokes executable code stored in a code field. In many FORTH systems, the tokens are addresses. However, tokens can take other forms depending on implementation. For example, Java, which is a variant of FORTH, uses byte tokens.

There are two types of FORTH commands: primitive FORTH commands having machine code in their code fields, and compound FORTH commands having token lists in their code fields.

The FORTH interpreter processes lists of commands in text strings. A list of FORTH commands contains a sequence of strings representing FORTH commands, separated by white spaces and terminated by a carriage return. The interpreter parses out commands in the text strings into tokens and executes code represented by these tokens. When the FORTH interpreter encounters a primitive command, it executes the machine code in its code field. When it encounters a compound command, it processes the token list in its code field. How it processes the token list depends upon how tokens are defined and implemented.

The text interpreter operates in two modes: interpreting mode and compiling mode. In the interpreting mode, a list of command names is interpreted; i.e., commands are parsed and executed. In the compiling mode, a list of command names is compiled; i.e., commands are parsed and corresponding tokens are compiled into a token list. This token list is given a name to form a new compound command, adding a new command record in the dictionary.

New compound commands are compiled to represent new token lists. This is the most powerful feature of FORTH, in that you can compile new compound commands, which replace lists of existing commands, both primitive and compound. The syntax to compile a new compound command is:

```
: <name> <list of existing commands> ;
```

Nested token lists are added as new compound commands until the final compound command becomes the solution of your problem. Lists are compiled and tested from the bottom up. The solution space can be explored wider and farther, and an optimized solution can be found more quickly.

Linear, sequential token lists are enhanced by control structures like branch structures and loop structures. A structure is a token list inside which the execution sequence can be modified dynamically. The following figure shows a sequential structure, a branch structure and a loop structure.

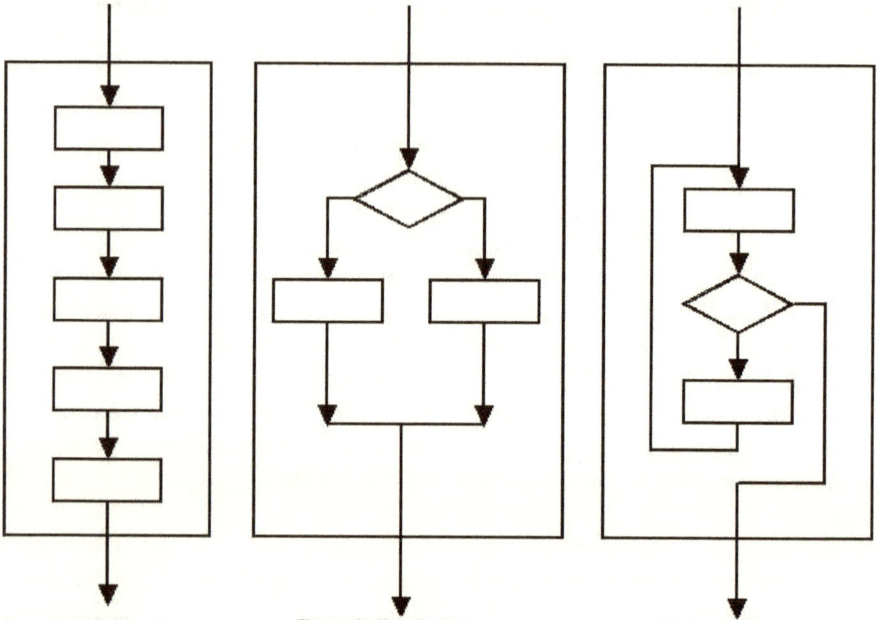

Sequential Structure Branch Structure Loop Structure

A structure has only one entry point and one exit point, although it may have many branches inside. Structures can be nested, but may not overlap with one another. A structure can therefore be considered an enhanced token. A compound command is a structure given a name.

Using the concept of structures, a new compound command has the following syntax:

```
: <name> <list of structures> ;
```

The fundamental reason why FORTH lists (command lists and token lists) can be simple, linear sequences of commands is that FORTH uses two stacks: a return stack to stored nested return addresses, and a parameter stack to pass parameters among nested commands. Parameters are passed implicitly on the parameter stack, and do not have to be explicitly invoked. Therefore, FORTH commands can be interpreted in a linear sequence, and tokens can be stored in simple, linear token lists. Language syntax is greatly simplified, internal representation of code is greatly simplified, and execution speed is greatly increased.

A FORTH Virtual Machine thus needs two stacks, efficient means to traverse nested token lists, and a CPU within a reasonable instruction set and memory device to support a small number of primitive commands. eForth is such an implementation which has been ported to many commercial microprocessors and microcontrollers. Auduino Uno with an ATmega328P microcontroller, is an ideal platform for an eForth implementation, 328eForth system.

1.3 FORTH for Firmware Development

To use FORTH to develop applications for ATmega328P with Arduino Uno, you have to have the following components:

First, you need a $29 Arduino Uno Board with an USB cable connecting to PC. Second, you also need a $34 AVRISP mkll In-System Programmer from Atmel to upload FORTH operating system to ATmega328P, and to configure ATmega328P.

The following picture shows my FORTH firmware development system: an Arduino Uno, an AVRISP mkll programmer, and a PC. Two USB cables connect Arduino Uno Boad and AVRISPmkll programmer to PC. The total cost besides the PC is $63.

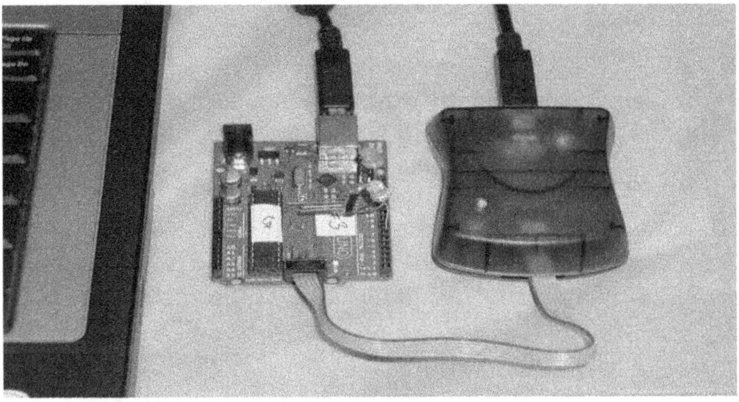

Third, on the PC, you need AVR Studio 4, an Integrated Development Environment (IDE) from Atmel Corp to assemble 328eForth. You can download it for free from www.atmel.com.

To upload FORTH into ATmega328P, you need AVRISP mkll which can write the flash memory, both the bootloader section and the application, in ATmega328P directly. There are a number of other programmers which can do it also. However, the best and the most reliable one is the AVRISP mkll from Atmel Corp. Of course, Atmel makes ATmega328P, and it made every effort to provide the best tool so that more people will use more of its chips.

Atmel also provides AVR Studio 4, an Integrated Development Environment (IDE) to assemble and compile source code written for Atmega328P, and other 8 bit microcontrollers it manufactures. It is free, but you have to register with Atmel before downloading it to your PC.

AVR Studio 4 contains an AVR assembler, C and C++ compilers, simulators, and debuggers. It also uploads assembled or compiled object code to ATmega328P through AVRISP mkll programmer. I only use the AVR assembler to assemble the source code of 328eForth, and then use AVRISP mkll to upload 328eForth object code to ATmega328P. Once 328eForth is uploaded to ATmega328P, all programming and debugging operations are performed from a terminal emulator on PC, through the USB cable connected to Arduino Uno.

On the PC, I use HyperTerminal to communicate with Arduino Uno. HyperTerminal comes with Windows, and can be accessed through \Start\All Programs\Accessories\Communication\HyperTerminal. Starting at Windows 7, Microsoft stopped bundling HyperTerminal with Windows. However, you can still download HyperTerminal application from MSDN website. The USB/COM driver enabling HyperTerminal to talk through the USB port to Arduino is located in the folder of C:\ arduino 0022\\drivers\FTDI drivers\. To load this driver, you need to download the Arduino 0022 system from www.arduino.cc.

There are other terminal emulators for PC to communication with Arduino. RealTerm can be downloaded from SourceForge (http://realterm.sourceforge.net/). It has many more options than HyperTerminal, but they work similarly.

You have to set up communication protocols on HyperTerminal or RealTerm so that they will communication with Arduino. The set up parameters are 19,200 baud, 1 start bit, 8 data bits, no parity, 1 stop bit, and no flow control.

Apart from the flash memory, ATmega328P also has what's called lock bits and fuse bytes, which are used to configure the chip to behave properly according to your requirements. The lock bits protect sections of flash memory from inadvertent reading and writing operations. The fuse bytes configure CPU, memory, and I/O devices and select modes of operations for these components. Lock bits and fuse bytes can be read and written under AVR Studio 4 system through AVRISP mkll programmer. These bits and bytes are configured properly for the ATmega328P chip on Arduino Uno and you do not have to worry about them. However, you may have to set these bits and bytes when you want to change the configuration of ATmega328P to do exactly what you what it to do, under conditions required by specific applications.

To develop programs for embedded systems, the conventional methodology is to write source code in C or in assembly. The source code is compiled or assembled. Object code is linked by a linker to produce execution code, which is uploaded to the target system. Now, you cross your fingers and turn on power. Most likely, the system does not work, and you enter into the debugging phase of development.

To debug a program in an embedded system, you need lots of sophisticated tools, like simulator, in-circuit emulator (ICE), an oscilloscope, and a good logic analyzer. You set up break points, and trace the microcontroller instructions cycle by cycle. It is very difficult when the application program is large and complicated, especially when you can only observe the microcontroller from the outside.

The Arduino 0022 development environment streamlines the programming process. You write your code in a sketch. You press the compile button to compile the sketch. Then, you cross your fingers and press the upload button. If it works, great for you. If it does not work, you are stuck. Arduino 0022 really cannot give you much help. If you do not have those sophisticated debugging tools I mentioned above, all you can do is go back to the source code, read it over and over again, and try to locate the bugs. Believe me. Debugging a large program without proper tools is not an easy job, on Arduino, or on any other microcontroller.

FORTH provides you the proper tools. You embed the debugging tools inside the microcontroller in the form of an interactive FORTH operating system. Source code in the form of many small commands is compiled by the target microcontroller in the embedded system. You can control the microcontroller from within, and observe its behavior from inside out. Break points are not necessary, because FORTH commands naturally break at their ends, and you can query their results interactively. New commands are compiled, tested, and debugged incrementally. The solution space can be explored quickly, and almost exhaustively. Reliable system can thus be built quickly. FORTH commands are lists of nested lists, and are very compact. Substantial applications can be stored in very small memory area.

1.4 Arduino Tao Board

Arduino Boards were designed to be expandable. The four sockets for I/O pins on board can take different daughter boards, or shields, which contain additional circuitry for various applications. The popularity of Arduino boards is in no small part due to the rich assortments of Arduino shields extending applications of Arduino boards to many different fields.

I am exploring Arduino boards in the opposite direction. What can I eliminate from Arduino Uno to build boards for custom application?

It is interesting that ATmega328P is housed in a 28 pin DIP package which can be removed and inserted into other DIP sockets. Now a days, most microcontrollers are packaged in narrow pin surface mount packages and are impossible to solder and unsolder. ATmega328P in a DIP package is very user friendly, and encourages hobbyists and students to use it in their projects.

The output pins on ATmega328P can each source or sink up to 40 mA of current, and they can be used to drive LED's directly. I found that a LED can be driven safely without a current limiting resistor. It is therefore very convenient to attach LED's directly to ATmega328P, although most experts advise that you should use current limiting resistors.

You can turn on a pull-up resistor when an I/O pin is configured for input. The resistance is 20-50 kΩ, depending on the power supply voltage. It is therefore very convenient to attach input sensors directly to input pins and use ATmega328P to drive the sensors, if they do not required large current.

Another interesting characteristic of ATmega328P is that its operating power supply voltage ranges from 1.8 V to 5.5 V, and its normal operating current is about 4 mA. It is therefore very convenient to drive this microcontroller with 2 AA batteries. Most AA batteries discarded from toys still have lots of charge to drive ATmega328P. These "exhausted" batteries still measure 1.4 volts. I had used a pair of AA batteries to power a application with ATmega328P, and had never changed the batteries for 4 months. The following picture shows that a bare ATmega328P chip sitting on a prototyping board driving an application with 2 AA batteries. The big black chip below ATmega328P is a TSOP32136, an infrared receiver for infrared communication.

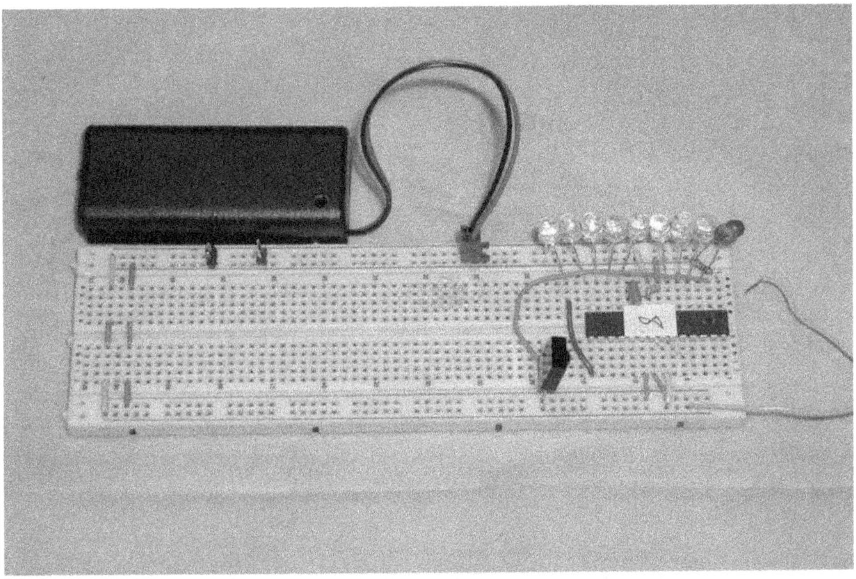

Here is another application where ATmega328P chip is mounted on a custom development board.

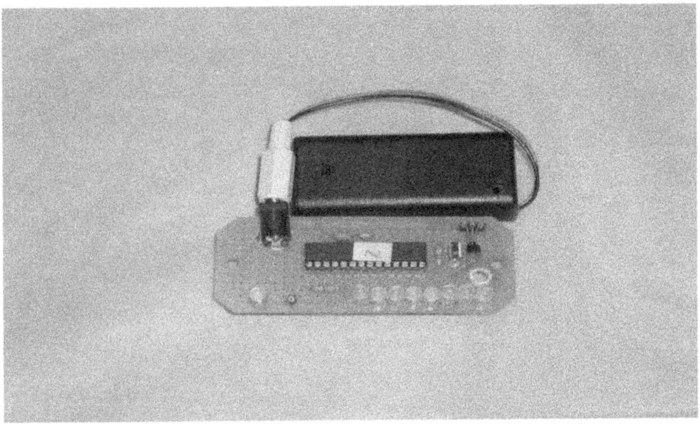

Arduino Uno has a 16 MHz crystal to drive the master oscillator in ATmega328P. ATmega328P can be configured to use many different oscillators. The one I am particularly interested is its 8 MHz internal oscillator. If you configure ATmega328P to run on the internal oscillator, you do not have to use an external crystal or resonator, and you gain two more pins for I/O operations. The internal oscillator is quite satisfactory for applications which do not require precise timing, and most casual application falls into this category.

The RESET pin (Pin 1) on ATmega328P has an internal pull-up resistor. Therefore, you really do not need an external pull-up resistor to the RESET pin. If you have a power switch on your application board, it service very well as a reset switch. If you use the power switch to reset ATmega328P, you can configure the chip so that you can use the RESET pin for I/O.

If you remove all the external components which are not necessary for the operation of ATmega328P, all you have to supply is power and ground, as shown in the following picture. The bare minimal connections are: Pins 7, 20 and 21 to Vcc power, and Pins 8 and 22 to ground. You don't even have to have a 0.1 uF bypass capacitor between power and ground. This configuration runs very reliably over long period of time. This is what I call Tao of Arduino, as shown in the following picture:

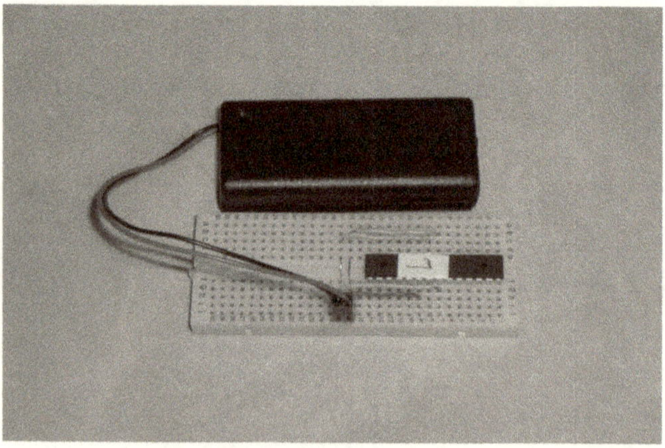

An application is built using the above Arduino Tao Board, as shown in the following picture:

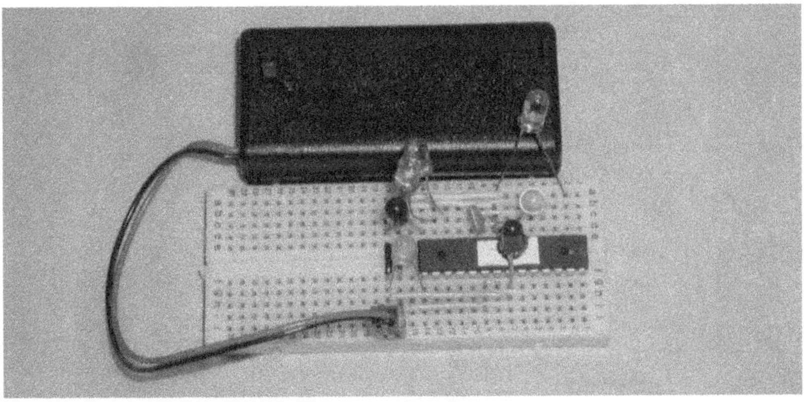

You can remove an ATmega328P from its socket on Arduino Uno, and plug it in you own board. Connect the RX (D0) and TX (D1) pins on Uno to Pins 2 and 3 of ATmega328P on your own board. Power up your board and 328eForth on ATmega328P will communicate with the terminal interface on PC through Arduino Uno (without its ATmega328P) and its USB cable. The following picture shows that you can control an ATmega328P on a target board through the communication pins on Arduino Uno from which the ATmega328P chip is removed.

This Arduino Tao Board has the following schematic diagram:

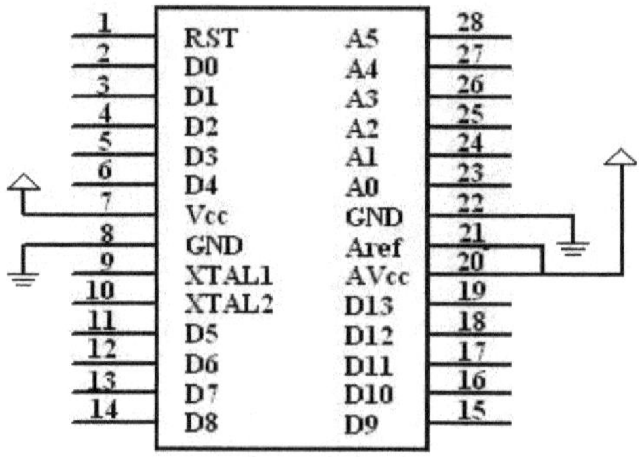

ATmega328P

As Loa Tzi said in Tao Te Ching:

For knowledge, add a little everyday.
For Tao (wisdom), delete a little everyday.
Delete and delete, until nothing is left.
With nothing, you can do everything.

--Lao Tzi, Tao Te Ching, Chapter 48

When you can make the ATmega328P microcontroller to work without the Arduino Uno Board, you have learnt everything about ATmega328P, and there is no problem you cannot solve, within the capability of ATmega328P. This is the Tao of Arduino.

Chapter 2. 328eForth for Arduino Uno

2.1 Introduction

For a very long time, firmware engineering meant to program a UV Erasable PROM chip and to insert it on a board which contained a microcontroller, some RAM memory chips, and some I/O chips, and a socket for the UV EPROM. Then flash memory chips replace UV EPROM's. And then everything is integrated into a single microcontroller chip, and we now have ISP, In System Programming, which allows you to program the microcontroller in its own socket. Arduino Uno integrates an ATmega328P microcontroller with all necessary hardware components on a small printed circuit board, and captures the fancy of a new generation of will-be firmware engineers and DIY hobbyists.

I admire the efforts Arduino developers put into this open hardware system, especially the simplification of the C programming language to these two statements:

setup(); loop();

These are the essence of firmware engineering. The only deficiency is the lack of interactivity between you and your microcontroller chip on the Arduino board. This is where FORTH can be of great help.

There is a very good FORTH system AmForth for Arduino Uno. You can download it from Source Forge http://sourceforge.net/projects/amforth/.

It follows the ANS FORTH Standard, but it has a few problems and does not behave exactly like the prevailing public domain FORTH systems, such as figFORTH, F83, FPC, and Win32FORTH. It is a fairly complicated implementation, involving hundreds of files in many different folders. ATmega328P is a lowly microcontroller, and does not deserve such a large supporting system to program it. After 20 years of implementing eForth on many different microcontrollers, I am certainly of the opinion that eForth is the FORTH best suited for this microcontroller. Nevertheless, AmForth is a good working FORTH system for ATmega328P. I studied it diligently and enjoyed reading its code.

The original eForth was implemented in Direct Thread Model by myself and Bill Muench. Dr. Richard Haskell implemented the first Subroutine Thread Model in 86se4th.asm for 8086 and 68000. I took his file and modified it so it could be assembled by the AVR assembler in AVR Studio 4 development system from Atmel. AmForth implemented many FORTH commands in AVR assembly, and these code were ported into my implementation. I call it 328eForth because it is configured specifically for ATmega328P, used on Arduino Uno.

The most important differences between 328eForth and AmForth are the following:

1. Subroutine Thread Model instead of the Direct Thread Model in AmForth.
2. Using byte addresses to access flash memory, which has native 16-bit cells.
3. All assembly code are in a single file, not scattered in hundreds of little files.
4. Flash programming is optimized through two 128 byte page buffers.
5. No interrupts and no multitasking.
6. EEPROM memory is not used.
7. Interpreter is in NRWW memory. Compiler and user extension are in RWW memory.
8. Ease in building turnkey applications

These differences make 328eForth much simpler, easier to use, to understand and to modify.

2.2 Installing Tools

Here are the steps you can follow to get everything running.

Get an Arduino Uno board from Jameco for about $29.

Get the Atmel AVR ISP mkII programmer from Mouser, for about $34.

Download the AVR Studio 4 from Atmel web site:
http://www.atmel.com/dyn/products/tools_card.asp?tool_id=2725

Install AVR Studio 4. Do not connect the AVR ISP mkII until the software installation is complete.

Studio 4 will install its driver, Jungo USB, for its AVR ISP mkII. The USB cable must not be connected until After the install in done.

Download the Arduino 0022 package at http://www.arduino.cc/en/Main/Software Unzip and install. This should load the USB to COM simulator from FTDI. The drivers are in that package at \Arduino-0022\drivers\FTDI drivers\.

To check on these USB drivers, go to
Start\Control-Panel\System\Hardware\Device-Manager and you will see Jungo\AVR ISP mkII. Under Ports (Com & LPT), you will see Arduino Uno (COM X).
Remember the COM port number X for use with HyperTerminal or RealTerm.

Download and install RealTerm from SourceForge
(http://realterm.sourceforge.net/). HyperTerminal is standard in Windows under Start\Accessories\Communication\, and it works similarly.

Connect the AVR ISP mkII ribbon cable to the six pin ISP header on Arduino Uno.
Red wire is #1 matching a tiny dot below the header, as shown in the picture below

Connect a USB cable to the AVR ISP mkII to the computer. Connect a USB cable from Arduino Uno to the computer. The AVR ISP MkII doesn't power the target so the Arduino USP is its power source. Check the serial connections as noted above.

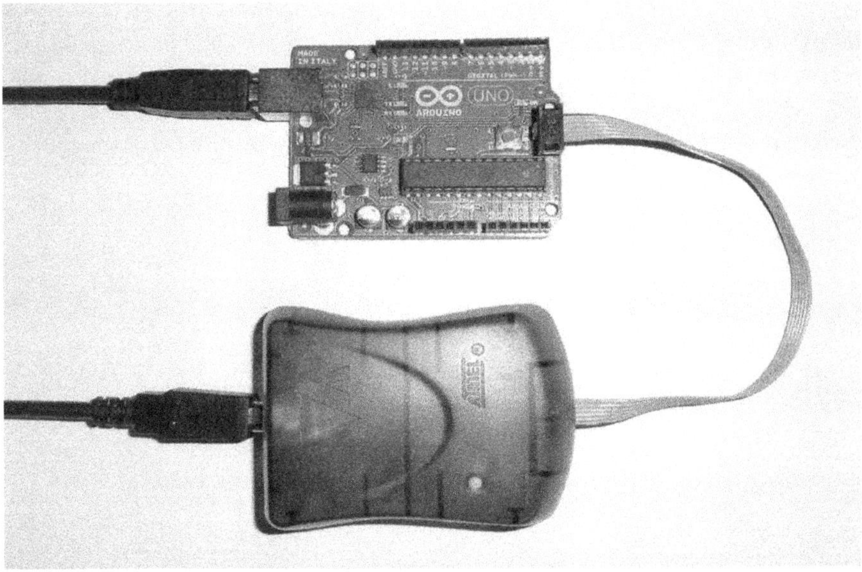

With the cables connected, you should be able to invoke arduino.exe in the Arduino 0022 folder, and do all the wonderful things with Arduino sketches.

You should also be able to invoke AVR Studio 4 and try out its features. I will use the AVR assembler in Studio 4 to assemble the 328eForth system, and then use AVR ISP mkll cable to upload 328eForth.hex to ATmega328P on Arduino Uno.

2.3 Assembling 328eForth

Start Atmel AVR Tools \AVR Studio 4\. In the pop-up window, select New Project. If you have used Studio 4 for other projects, you can select Project Wizard in the Project pull-down menu

In the Welcome to AVR Studio 4 Window, go to Project Type panel and select Atmel AVR Assembler. Enter a project name, like my_eforth, in the Project Name panel, The same name will appear in the Initial File panel. You can change this file name to the one you like.

A default path is shown in the Location panel. You can change this path by clicking the box to the right of Location panel, and then navigate to the folder you want.

Click the Next>> button and you are lead to a Debugger Platform and Device selection window. In the Debugger Platform panel, select AVR Assembler 2. In the Device Panel, select ATmega328P. Click Finish button and the Studio 4 Window shows you the new project, with an empty .asm file of the name (my_eforth) you chose above. You are ready to go to work.

Copy the entire contents of 328eForth.asm into this blank file my_eforth.asm.

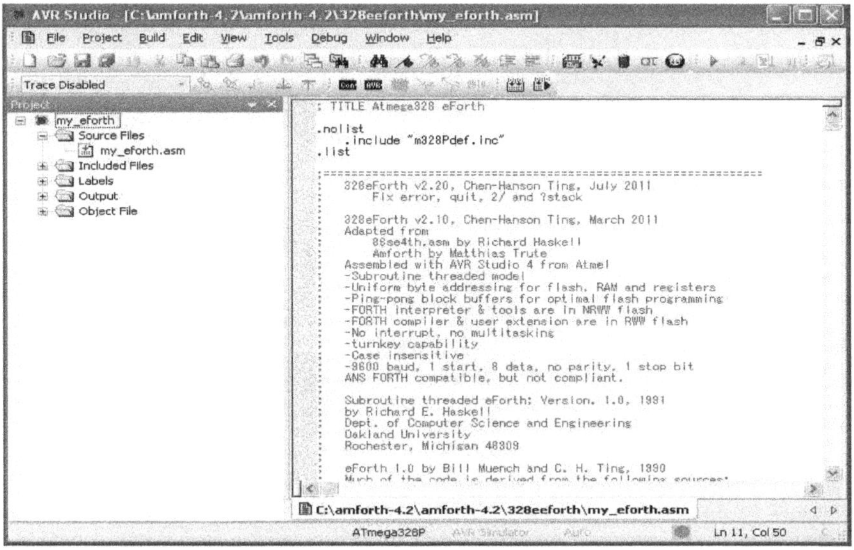

Pull down the Project Menu and select Assembler Options, and check the Create List File box. This way the assembler will produce a listing file for my_eforth, if you care to look at the assembled code. It is always nice to see actual code the assembler produces.

Now is the time for the big show. Pull down Build menu and select the Build button. Studio 4 starts assembling my_eforth.asm, and displays lots of messages in the Build panel at the bottom of the big window. Its final message is: "Assembly complete. 0 errors. 84 warnings" The assembler does not like 328eForth commands with names of even number of bytes, because it has to append extra null bytes to the cell boundaries. There are 84 of these commands. It also reports that the assembled system has 3560 bytes of code, 1596 bytes of data, and the total byte count is 5156.

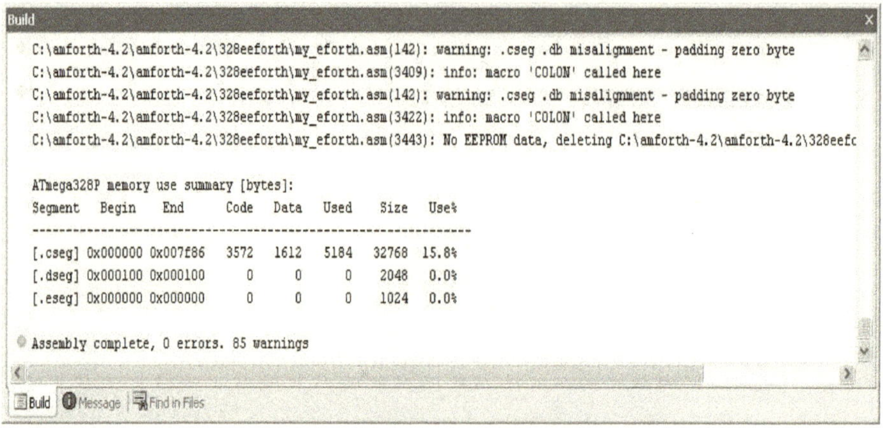

Before you upload my_eforth to the Arduino Uno for testing, it is an educational experience to simulate my_eforth with the AVR simulator. Pull down Debug menu and select Start Debugging option. The simulator shows you a bewildering set of windows and panels, displaying information on CPU registers, program memory, data memory, and I/O registers. Focus on the Editor panel showing the assembly file. A yellow arrow is pointing to the beginning of execution code at memory location 0, with the instruction JMP ORIG.

Press F11 to single step through a few lines of start-up code. That's all I can tell you about the AVR simulator. If you want to change 328eForth.asm, this is the best and only tool you will need to debug it.

Pull down Debug menu and select Stop Debugging option. You will be back to AVR Studio 4.

In the second row of icons you can see two icons that look like integrated circuits. Click on the left one labeled CON, and the Connection Dialog window appears. Check AVRISP mkII on the left and USB on the right. Then click Connect. You will then be taken to the AVRISP window. If not, click on the bug icon to the right labeled AVR.

On the AVRISP window, select Main page. In the Device and Signature Bytes panel, pick ATmega328P in the Device box. In the Programming and Target Settings panel, you will see that the ISP Frequency is set to 1 MHz. Click the Erase Device and Read Signature buttons to verify that you can erase the chip and read its signature bytes.

If AVRISP failed to erase ATmega328P or read the signature bytes, click the Settings button, and lower the ISP frequency to probably 125 kHz.

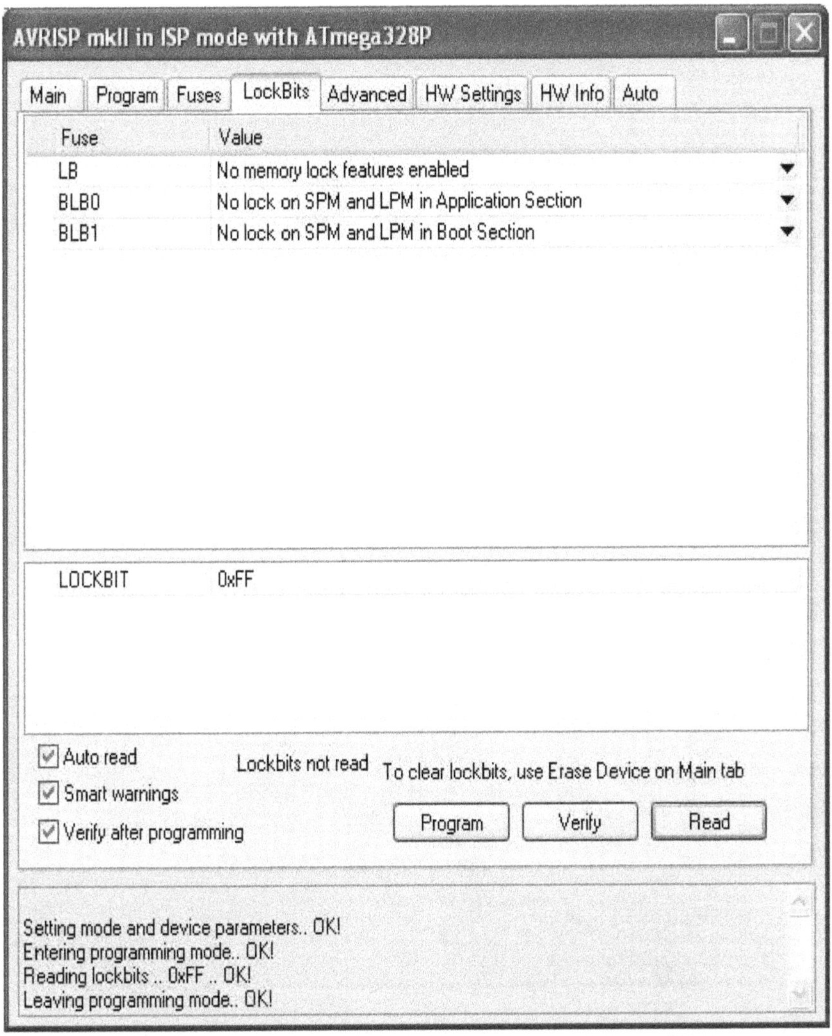

Select the Lock Bits page. ATmega328P also has what's called lock bits and fuse bytes, which are used to configure the chip to behave properly according to your requirements. The lock bits protect sections of flash memory from inadvertent reading and writing operations. Select 0xFF for the lock bits to allow writing to the flash memory. Click Program button to program the lock bits.

Select the Fuses page. The fuse bytes configure CPU, memory, and I/O devices and select modes of operations for these components. Select 0xFD for the Extended Fuse byte, 0xD8 for the High Fuse byte, and 0xFF for the Low Fuse byte. Click Program button to program the fuse bytes.

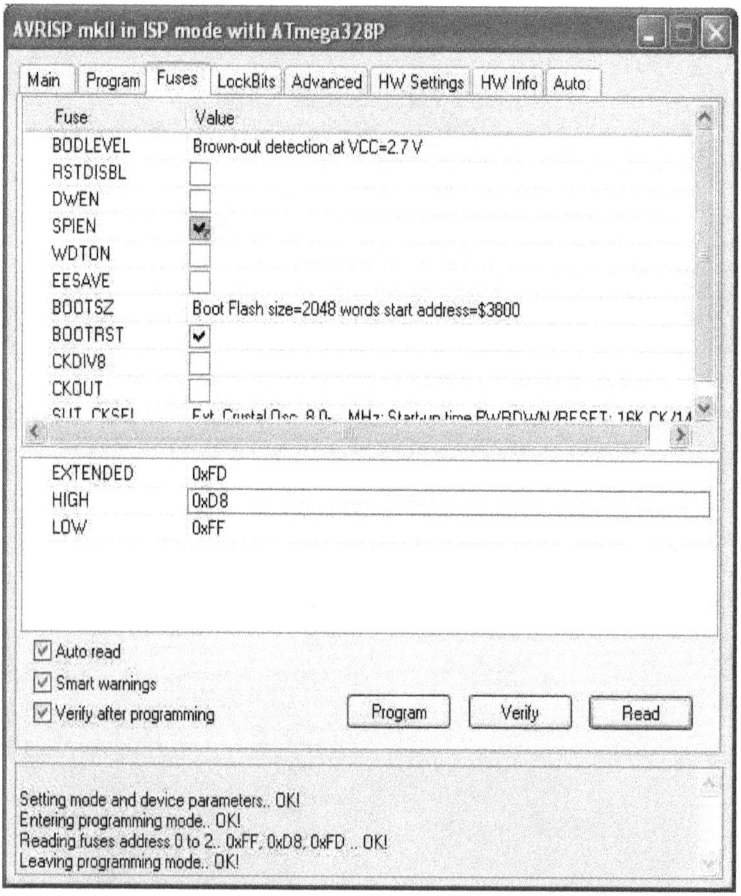

Select the Program page. In the Device panel, check the box labeled "Erase device before flash programming." In the Flash panel, open and navigate to your my_eforth hex image in your project folder.

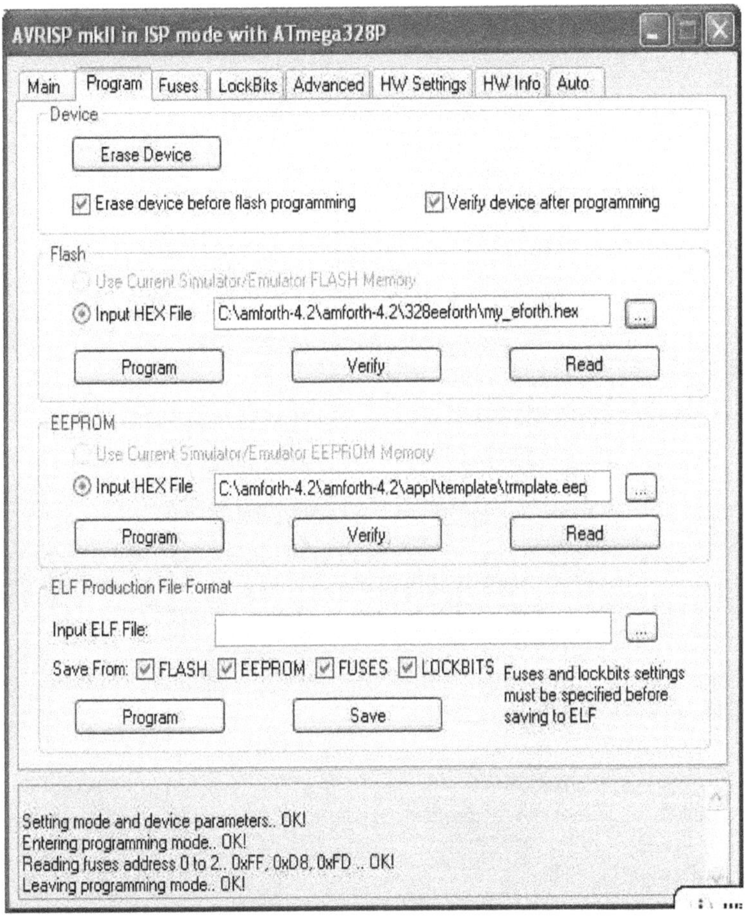

Your should now have the green power LED lit on the Arduino Uno. The green LED lit inside AVR ISP MkII case (shows USB OK) and the green LED lit (shows programmer cable OK) on the surface of the AVR ISP MkII.

Click the Program button in the Flash panel. You will see a dialog at the lower left as the program is loaded. You may now disconnect the AVR ISP mkII programmer. However I generally keep it connected in case I have to reload 328eForth.

2.4 The Terminal Interface

After 328eForth is loaded through the AVRISP programmer, you switch on the USB/COM port supported by the HyperTerminal interface program (located in Windows Accessories). Load HyperTerminal or Realterm, and you can now talk to 328eForth on Arduino Uno.

On the HyperTerminal console pull down the Call menu and select Disconnect option. Then, pull down the File menu and select Properties option. In the Connect Using dialog box, select the COM port you saw earlier in the USB device assignment. Click the Configuration button and a COMx Properties window pops up. Select 19,200 baud, 8 data bits, no parity, 1 stop bit, and no flow control. Then click OK button to dismiss the COMx Properties window.

In the main Properties window, click on the Settings tab and the click the ASCII Setup button, and an ASCII Setup window pops up. Enter 900 in the Line Delay dialog box to insert 900 msec delay after sending each line of text. Later you will download source code files and you will need this end of line delay.

Click OK button to dismiss the ASCII Setup window. Click OK button in the main Properties window and dismiss this window also.

Now you are back to the HyperTerminal Console window. Pull down Call menu and select Call option, and you will see the sign-on message generated by 328eForth:

328eForth v2.20

Hitting Return key several times, and you should see the two send/receive LEDs flash on Arduino Uno, and ok messages are displayed on the HyperTerminal console.
You can now type in FORTH commands to interact with 328eForth on Arduino Uno.

328eForth is case insensitive. You can type commands in either upper or lower case.

2.5 Testing 328eForth on Arduino Uno

To recapitulate, you have to install AVR Studio 4, and Arduino 0022. You have to connect your Arduino Uno board to a USB port on your PC, and a AVR ISP mkII programmer to Arduino Uno and to another USB port. Assemble 328eForth.asm, and upload its .hex file to Arduino Uno. Open HyperTerminal on your Windows and you get the sign-on message:

```
328eForth v2.20
```

Type these FORTH commands to test the system:

```
words  100 dump
200 idump
7000 idump
```

Note that 32eForth is in the hexadecimal base when it starts.

After bring up 328eForth, type WORDS and you will see a list of eForth commands on the HyperTerminal console:

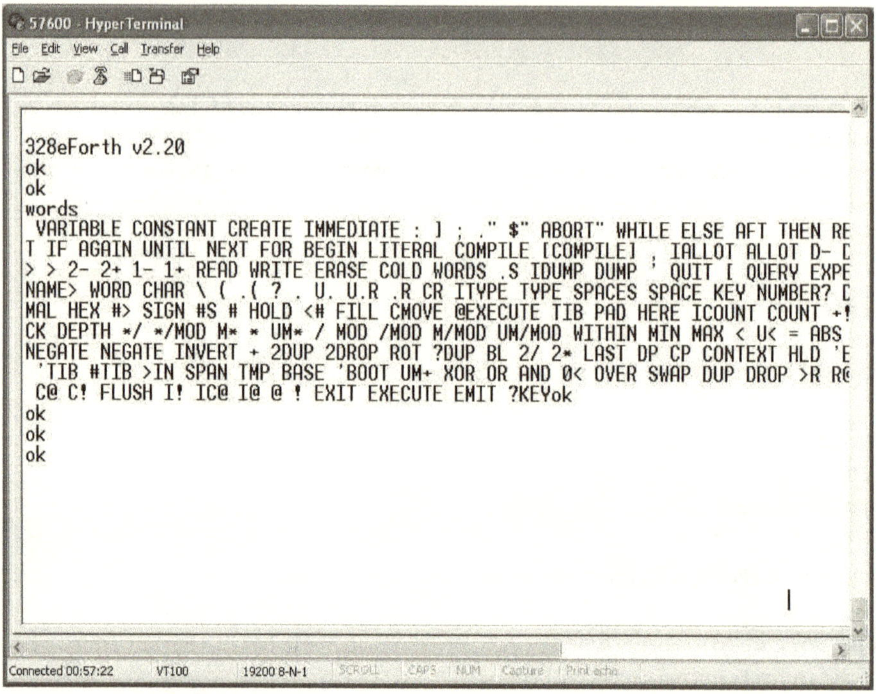

HyperTerminal breaks up a word at the right margin of the window console. You will have to read across lines to see whole words. There are 151 FORTH commands visible in 328eForth system. There are actually about 200 eForth commands, but many of them are hidden, without link and name fields. These hidden commands are needed to implement the 328eForth system, but are not useful in normal programming. Therefore, I commented out their link fields and name fields in the assembly source file. If you are interested in how 328eForth was implemented, and perhaps like to modify it, you can go into the 328eForth.asm file and remove the commenting ';' characters before the COLON macro's. Re-assemble, and you will see all the commands, and you can invoke them from your new dictionary.

These 151 visible commands are documented in the Appendix for your reference.

Make sure that HyperTerminal inserts a 900 ms delay after sending each line of text. Then, you can download a text file by pulling down Transfer Menu and select Send Text File option. From the file selection window, select a file and push the Open button. Or, double clicking the selected file. Text from the selected file will be sent to 328eForth, one line at a time, and you will see how 328eForth responds to these lines.

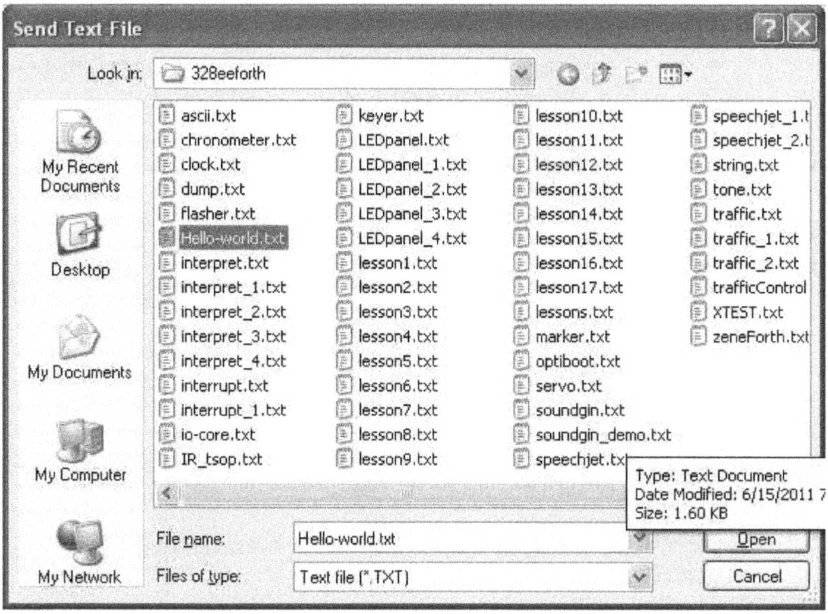

Bill Ragsdale had written for a set of demo applications for Arduino with AmForth. I modified these files so that they work properly under 328eForth. To test them, download and test the following files in this order:

File	**Function**
hello-world.txt	The universal greeting
marker.txt	Tools to delete commands and reload files
io-core.txt	Core commands to read and write IO registers
flasher.txt	Blink on-board LED
tone.txt	Generate audio tones
keyer.txt	Morse code practice kit
chronometer.txt	A stopwatch to measure time to execute a command.

dump.txt	A smart dump program to display RAM and flash memory.

Bill put in lots of comments in these files. Read them carefully and follow his instructions to test the application commands. After a file is downloaded, there are usually a list of commands that you can type in to see how things work.

After downloading flasher.txt, you can type these commands:

```
DECIMAL \ so that 1000 MS delays for 1 sec  1000
3 MANY  \ flash Digital Line 13 LED 3 times,
        \ on 1 sec, off 1 sec.
```

After downloading keyer.txt, you can type these commands:

```
V       \ dit dit dit dah
SOS     \ distress signal
```

Of course, it assumes that you have a speaker connected to Digital Line D6, and can generate an audio tone with these commands.

After downloading dump.txt, you can use Bill's smart DUMP command as follows:

```
HEX
100 80 RAM DUMP
7000 100 FLASH DUMP
```

There is no FORGET, which trims back the dictionary, as continually coordinating allocation in two address spaces is difficult. In the marker.txt file, Bill defined a defining command MARKER, that compiles a command that will trim the dictionary back to a starting point. Use it as:

```
   marker chop-point
```

Later executing

```
chop-point  will act like:
  forget chop-point
```

Bill generally begins his code modules with:

```
chop-XX  marker chop-XX
```

The first chop-XX will cause an unknown command error and then marker creates it again. Later recompilations will execute the first chop-XX cutting back the dictionary and then replace the chop-XX command.

2.6 Learning More about eForth

If you are new to the FORTH programming language, or has some prior knowledge on a different FORTH system, you may want to look into a series of tutorials I prepared for the earlier eForth systems. There are 17 lessons in that many text files. Your are encourage to take these lessons and type in the commands. You can also download these files in HyperTerminal, and then type in the final commands to test loaded applications. These lessonXX.txt files are included in the distribution package with 328eForth.asm.

The contents of these lesson files are listed in the following table:

Lesson	**Contents**
1	Hello, World!
2.	Big characters
3.	Forth Interest Group
4.	Repeated patterns
5	The theory that Jack built
6	Help
7	Money exchange
8	Temperature conversion
9	Weather reporting
10	Multiplication table
11	Calendars
12	Sines and cosines
13	Square roots
14	Number conversion
15	ASCII character table
16	Random numbers
17	Guess a number

Chapter 3. What eForth Does But Arduino Cannot

What can eForth do over and above Arduino 0022?

One quick answer I can give you is to ask you typing in the following command:

```
0 DUMP
80 DUMP
```

and you will see the following display in the HyperTerminal console:

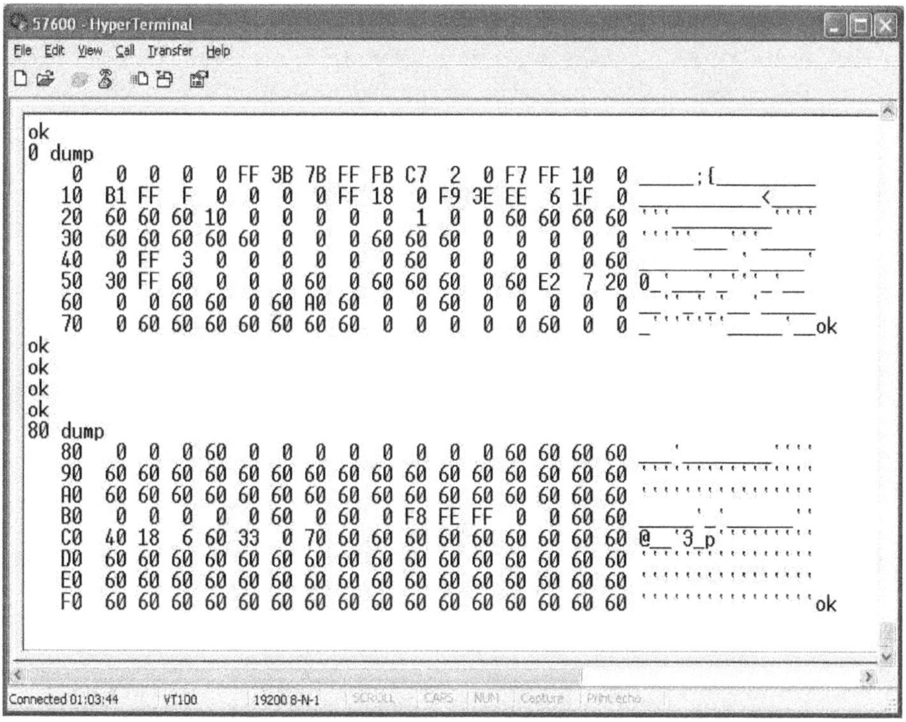

In this display, you see the RAM memory of ATmega328P from location 0 to location $FF. If you had read the AVR Microcontroller Data Book, you would know that the first 32 bytes are 32 registers in ATmega CPU, the next 64 bytes from $20 to $5F are the I/O registers, and the last 160 bytes from $60 to $FF are Extended I/O registers. Many of these registers are not implemented as physical devices, and they show up containing $60. Actual I/O registers show their actual contents.

You can examine the contents of every CPU and I/O register any time. You cannot do it in Arduino.

Even better, you can change the contents of the CPU and I/O registers! As the CPU registers are used by the 328eForth system, I do not recommend your changing them without knowing exactly what you are doing. You can easily crash the system if you advertently change some of the critical CPU registers. However, there is no better way to learn the I/O devices in ATmega328P than to study the register definitions and functions of the bits in these registers, and to change these bits while observing the signals coming out of the corresponding I/O pins.

Once you understand the control, status, and data registers in an I/O device, you can write a short FORTH command to exercise this device the way you eventually will use it. This command to test the device will grow to be a part of your application.

In the following sections, I will show you how to change some of the I/O registers directly with C! commands, to operate these I/O devices. You need that thick 566 page AVR Microcontroller Data Boot opened on your computer, and read the register definitions to follow the discussions. I will show you addresses of the I/O registers, but you will have to look up the definitions of bits in these registers to go along. It is difficult at first to read register addresses and contents in hex, but I hope you will get used to them. It will be very rewarding when you see that these bits actually work and produce results you can observe visually.

The best way to wade through this thick Data Book is to test the devices interactively with 328eForth.

Are you ready?

3.1 USART

The first device I will discuss is the serial USART0 port, because it is the only I/O device used by 328eForth. It has the following set of registers:

Address	Register	Name	Function	Initial Value
$C0	UCSR0A	Control and status register A	Status of transmitter and receiver	--
$C1	UCSR0B	Control and status register B	Interrupt, enabling, data format	$18
$C2	UCSR0C	Control and status register C	Mode select, start, stop, parity	$6
$C4	UBRR0L	Baud rate register low	Baud rate divisor, low byte	$33
$C5	UBRR0H	Baud rate register high	Baud rate divisor, high byte	0
$C6	UDR0	Data register	Transmitted or received data	--

UCSR0A reports the current status of the USART0 and UDR0 contains transmitted or received data. These registers change dynamically and do not require initialization. UCSR0B/C selects 1 start bit, 8 data bits, 1 stop bit, no parity and no flow control. The UBRR0L/H registers set USART0 up to run at 19,200 baud. Do not change these 4 registers unless you know what you are doing. If you mess up these registers, Arduino Uno will not talk to the HyperTerminal and you have to reach for the reset button.

Read AVR Data Book to learn what each bit in UCSR0B/C is doing. You can understand these bits better when you are actually looking at them on the HyperTerminal console.

One easy experiment you can do is to change the baud rate register UBBR0L from

$33 to $66 by typing the following commands:

```
$66 $C4 C!
```

If you are in hexadecimal mode, you do not have to type the $ prefix before numbers:

```
HEX 66 C4 C!
```

The baud rate is changed from 19,200 baud to 9,600 baud. Now, HyperTerminal stops talking to Arduino. Pull down Call menu and select Disconnect option. Pull down File menu and select Properties option. In the Properties window, change the baud rate to 9,600 baud. Connect the phone line, and Arduino will talk to HyperTerminal at 9,600 baud.

Type '0 DUMP' commands, and you will see that contents of UBRR0L register at C4 is changed to 66.

Type the following commands to get back to 19,200 baud:

```
33 C4 C!
```

Change the baud rate of HyperTerminal back to 19,200 baud so Arduino will talk again.

Always return HyperTerminal to 19,200 baud. Otherwise, when Arduino Uno is reset and reverts to 19,200 baud, you would spend a long time wondering why Arduino does not talk to the HyerTerminal. It could cause a panic, if you forget that they are using different baud rates.

3.2 GPIO Port B

The Digital I/O Line 13 on Arduino Uno is connected to bit-5 of GPIO Port B, PB-5. Port B as a general purpose I/O device has the following registers:

Address	Register	Name	Function	Initial Value
$23	PINB	Input register	Status of input pins	--
$24	DDRB	Direction register	1: output; 0: input	0
$25	PORTB	Data register	Output data, pull-up resistor	0

Setting a bit in DDRB register makes the corresponding pin an output pin. Then, writing this bit in PORTB register sends it to the output pin. It is very easy to turn the LED connected to Line 13 on and off by the following commands:
HEX

```
20  24  C!   \ make Line 13 an output pin
20  25  C!   \ turn Line 13 LED on
0   25  C!   \ turn Line 13 LED off
```

If you read AVR Data Book carefully, you will find that when a pin is set up as an output pin, writing a 1 to that bit in PINB register will toggle this output pin. Try the following commands and you can verify this function:

```
20  23  C!   \ toggle Line 13 LED
20  23  C!   \ toggle Line 13 LED
```

Type '0 DUMP' commands and you can see the current state of these registers as you turn the LED on and off.

Now, we can replicate what the BLINK sketch example does in Arduino 0022. Here is the program in FORTH:

```
: MS ( n -- ) FOR AFT $1CB FOR NEXT THEN NEXT ;
: BLINK 20 24 C! BEGIN 20 23 C! 400 MS AGAIN ;
FLUSH
BLINK
```

400 in hexadecimal equals to 1024 in decimal. $400 MS will cause a delay of about 1 second. Execute BLINK will cause the Line 13 LED to blink forever.

BLINK sketch is the first program every Arduino user runs It gives you a warm and fuzzy feeling that you are making Arduino Uno do something significant. However, the above FORTH BLINK program is the silliest program a FORTH programmer can ever write. It is an infinite loop you cannot get out, unless you push the reset button or pull the power plug off. The ATmega328P microcontroller is not made to run BLINK. It is much more powerful and much more intelligent than just turning a stupid LED on and off.

A thoughtful FORTH programmer would write this program instead:

```
: BLINK 20 24 C! BEGIN 20 23 C! 400 MS ?KEY UNTIL  DROP ;
FLUSH
BLINK
```

This program will blink the LED forever as the earlier one. But, when you are tired of looking at this stupid LED, you can stop it by pressing any key on the keyboard. You can exit the loop. Now, you can type in other commands to the 328eForth system, and do other useful things.

328eForth is you friend. It can help you explore the wonderful world of ATmega328P.

If a bit in DDRB is cleared to 0, the corresponding pin becomes an input pin. Initially this input pin is tri-stated. If you set the corresponding bit in PORTB register to a 1, this input pin will be pulled to Vcc by an internal pull-up resister. This pull-up resister is very useful and it simplifies the external circuitry of many input devices. For example, you can connect this input pin to a push-button switch with its other terminal grounded. If the switch is open, you will read a high on the input pin, because of the pull-up resister. If the switch is closed, you will read a low on the input pin.

Try this on Digital I/O Line 8, which is connected to Bit-0 in Port B. Type the following commands to test the switch:

```
24  C!   \ make all Port B pins input
25  C!   \ turn on pull-up resistor for Line 8
23  C@  .  \ read PINB port and show its contents
23 C@  .   \ repeat with switch on and off
```

3.3 Timer/Counter0 and Tone Generator

ATmega328P has three very powerful, and hence complicated, timer/counters. They can be used as timers, counters, pulse width modulators, and square wave generators. Timer/Counter0 and Timer/Counter2 have an 8 bit counter registers, and Timer/counter1 has a 16 bit counter register. Here we will follow Bill Ragsdale's tone generator example in tone.txt file, and use Timer/Counter0 to generator audio tones.

Timer/Counter0 had the following registers:

Address	**Register**	**Name**	**Function**	**Initial Value**
$44	TCCR0A	Control register A	Mode select	0
$45	TCCR0B	Control register B	Clock select	0
$46	TCNT0	Count register	Counter value	0
$47	OCR0A	Output compare register A	Compare value. When equal to TCNT0, generate output on OC0A	0
$48	OCR0B	Output compare register B	Compare value. When equal to TCNT0, generate output on OC0B	0

The bits in Control Registers A and B are complicated, and you have to read the AVR Data Book to understand them. To run Timer/Counter0 as a free run counter, set it up in the CTC (Clear Timer on Compare Match) mode. Store a value in OCR0A register to specify the period of the audio tone. Connect a speaker to Digital I/O Line 6, which is on Bit 6 in Port D, PD-6, and is toggles by the output compare signal of OC0A. Here are the commands you have to type:

```
HEX
```

```
40  2A  C!    \ make OC0A (I/O Line 6, PD-6)
              \ an output pin
42  44  C!    \ toggle OC0A on compare match,
              \ CTC mode
FF  47  C!    \ maximum count in OCR0A to compare
3   45  C!    \ select /64, prescaler=3,
              \ start counter
```

You will hear a tone from the speaker, if everything is set up correctly. To turn off the speaker, type:

```
0   45  C!      \ prescaler=0, no clock to
                \ timer/counter0
```

Storing a value from 1 to 5 into TCCR0B changes the prescaler between the master clock and Timer/Counter0. Each step in the prescaler increases the prescaler divisor by a factor of 4 or 8, and you can hear the tone pitch changes drastically. To make smaller changes in the tone pitch, change the value in OCR0A register at location $47.

Arduino Uno has a master clock of 16 MHz. With a /64 prescaler, the clock to Timer/Counter0 is 250 KHz. With a divisor of 255 in OCR0A register, the pitch we get from OCR0A is about 490 Hz. You can play with the prescaler and the value in OCR0A to get different pitches.

Now, let us try to run Timer/Counter0 as a PMW (Pulse Width Modulator) device. Remove the speaker from Digital I/O Line 6, and connect an LED to it. The anode pin (long leg) is connected to Line 6, and the cathode (short leg) is connected to ground. Type in the following commands:

```
HEX
40  2A  C!    \ I/O Line 6 is set up as an output pin
83  44  C!    \ TCCR0A, fast, non-inverting PWM mode
80  47  C!    \ set OCR0A to mid-range
3   45  C!    \ prescaler=3, start PWM
```

The LED will be turn on to medium brightness. Reduce the brightness by typing:

```
10  47  C!    \ decrease LED brightness
```

Increase the brightness by typing:

```
F0  47  C!    \ increase LED brightness
```

Now change to the fast, inverting PWM mode:

```
C3  44  C!    \ inverting PWM mode
```

PWM output is now inverted. Storing a bigger value in OCR0A reduces LED brightness. Storing a smaller value in OCR0A increases LED brightness.

If you have an oscilloscope, you can watch the PWM waveforms. Then, you will really appreciate the ease in using 328eForth to control your hardware.

You can change the PWM to the phase correct mode by typing:

```
81  44  C!    \ non-inverting phase correct PWM mode or,
C1  44  C!    \ inverting phase correct PWM mode
```

Changing the count value in OCR0A and the prescaler in TCCR0B, you can experiment with Timer/Counter0 to you heart's delight. You need an oscilloscope to see the waveforms, and preferably some servo motors to really see the PWM output doing real work.

The base frequency of the fast PWM oscillator is:

Prescaler	Base Frequency
1	31.2 KHz
2	7.81 KHz
3	980 Hz
4	244 Hz
5	61 Hz

3.4 Timer/Counter1

Timer/Counter1 has a 16-bit counter which offers wider dynamic range and higher accuracy in timing/counting. It is also more complicated than Timer/Counter0 and 2. Nevertheless, their operations are very similar. Bill Ragsdale wrote a chronometer program to measure execution time of FORTH code, and I like to reproduce this measuring function with Timer/Counter1.

The registers and their functions in Timer/Counter1 are as follows:

Address	Register	Name	Function	Initial Value
$80	TCCR1A	Control register A	Mode select	0
$81	TCCR1B	Control register B	Mode and clock select	0
$84	TCNT1L	Count register Low	Counter value low byte	0
$85	TCNT1H	Count register High	Counter value high byte	0
$88	OCR1AL	Output compare register A Low	Compare low byte. When equal to TCNT1, generate output on OC1A	0
$89	OCR1AH	Output compare register A High	Compare high byte.	0

You first clear TCCR1A to set up Timer/Counter1 in the normal counting mode. To time an event, you clear the 16-bit counter TCNT1 and store a prescaler value into TCCR1B to start the counter. After the event, clear TCCR1B to stop the counter. Then, read the accumulated counts in TCNT1 counter.

Before doing all these things, let us first download the marker.txt to compile the MS function. Then, type in the following commands:

```
HEX
 0 80  C!     \ clear TCCR1A to set up
              \ normal counting mode
0  84  !      \ clear 16-bit counter TCNT1
5  81  C!  100 MS  0  81  C!
              \ time '100 MS' commands
84  ?         \ read counts in TCNT1 counter
```

Let us stay in hexadecimal base, and 100 MS delays for 256 milliseconds. 400 MS delays for 1.024 seconds. My experiments show that '0 MS' takes $220 counts, '100 MS' takes 1262 counts, and '400 MS' takes $4322 counts. They look right to me.

With a prescaler of 5, Timer/Counter1 overflows at about 4 seconds, while Time/Counter0 would overflow at about 16 milliseconds. To generate waves at 1 Hz range, you have to use Timer/Counter1. We can blink a LED at 1 second periods using Timer/Counter1, if we connect a LED to the compare output pin OC1A, which is the Digital I/O Line 9, or PB-1 port.

```
HEX
2      24  C!    \ set DDRB PB-1 (Line 9)
                 \ as output pin
40     80  C!    \ set Timer/Counter1
                 \ to CTC mode
8000   88  !     \ init OCR1A compare register
                 \  to a value
B      81  C!    \ CTC mode, prescaler=3,
                 \ start wave
```

Changing the prescaler/mode value in TCCR1B changes the frequency of the output wave. The frequency and value in TCCR1B are shown as follows:

TCCR1B Value	Prescaler	Divisor	Frequency
9	1	1	244 Hz
A	2	8	30.5 Hz
B	3	64	3.75 Hz
C	4	256	0.96 Hz
D	5	1024	0.24 Hz

3.5 ADC – Analog to Digital Converter

Analog to Digital Converter is the most interesting, and probably the most complicated device in a microcontroller. In ATmega328P chip, we have 6 channels of ADC to read analog signals from external circuits, making it extremely useful for real applications looking at real analog signals. From a programmer's point of view, its ADC is not very complicated, and we only have to worry about the following 5 registers:

Address	Register	Name	Function	Initial Value
$78	ADCL	Data register Low	Data low byte	0
$79	ADCH	Data register High	Date high byte	0
$7A	ADCSRA	Control register A	Control, status, and prescaler bits	0
$7B	ADCSRB	Control register B	Auto-triggering source	0
$7C	ADMUX	Multiplexer selection register	Voltage reference and multiplexer section	0

ATmega328P has an internal temperature sensor, connected to Channel 8 of the ADC device. In addition, the internal 1.1 V reference voltage is connected to Channel 14, and a ground is connected to Channel 15. These Channels are very useful in testing the ADC.

Using 5 V power for reference and measuring the internal 1.1 V source, set up the ADMUX register and start the conversion this way:

```
HEX
4E  7C  C!    \ select 5 V reference;
              \ select Channel 14
C3  7A  C!    \ enable/start ADC;
              \ select /8 prescaler
78  ?         \ display results, nominally $E0
```

For reasons I do not understand, a prescaler less than 3 would not start ADC conversion in this mode of operation. The following commands measures the ground on Channel 15:

```
4F  7C  C!     \ 5 V reference;
               \ ground input on Channel 15
C3  7A  C!     \ start conversion
78  ?          \ display results, 0
```

The temperature sensor is connected to Channel 8, and it is recommended in AVR Data Book to read it with the internal 1.1 V source for reference. Type the following commands:

```
C8  7C  C!     \ C selects 1.1 V reference;
               \ 8 selects temperature sensor
C3  7A  C!     \ starts conversion
78  ?          \ displays results,
               \ nominally $160
```

If you connect an external analog signal source to the A0 pin, then type the following commands to read its analog value:

```
1  27  C!     \ setup A0 as input pin,
              \ which is on PC-0 port
1  28  C!     \ turn on pull-up resister
              \ on A0 pin
40  7C  C!    \ setup reference and
              \ multiplexer inputs
C3  7A  C!    \ start conversion
78  ?         \ display results
```

3.6 Build a Turnkey Application

In the FORTH parley, 'Turnkey' means configuring a FORTH system so that when power is applied and the system boots up, it initializes all the hardware devices in the system and start to execute the application it was designed to run. In 328eForth, you write lots of new commands. These commands are used to build more power commands until the last command looks like this:

: APPL SETUP BEGIN READ-INPUTS SEND-OUTPUTS AGAIN ;

To turnkey this application so that it executes APPL command on booting-up, type the following commands:

```
 ' APPL 'BOOT !   \ store address of APPL
                  \ in variable 'BOOT
$100 ERASE        \ erase flash
$100 $100 WRITE \ save RAM $100-17F
                  \ to flash $100-17F
$180 ERASE        \ erase flash if this
                  \ page is used
$180 $180 WRITE \ save RAM $180-1FF
                  \ to flash $180-1FF
```

Now, the ATmega328P has the 328eForth system with the complete application saved to the flash memory. When the Arduino Uno is reset or powered up, APPL will run.

Actually, after APPL command is compiled, all FORTH commands are already stored in the flash memory, but all the variables are still in RAM. Assuming that necessary data in RAM that have to be saved are between RAM locations from $100 to $1FF, the WRITE commands above save them all to the flash memory from $100 to $1FF. When 328eForth boots up, it automatically copies these two pages from flash to RAM, and APPL will start with all the necessary data in RAM.

With this limitation that you can save and restore only 256 bytes of RAM memory, you can build any turnkey application for Arduino Uno.

Chapter 4. Features in 328eForth Implementation

4.1 Addressing Memory

Flash memory in ATmega microcontrollers is organized in 16-bit cells. This allows addressing to the full 128 Kbyte flash memory with 16 bit addresses. In ATmega328P the flash memory runs from cell address hex 0000 to 3FFF or decimal 0 to 16,383. RAM and EEPROM memories are byte addressed.

In 328eForth, I chose to address flash memory in bytes, so that it is easier to move data between flash memory and RAM memory. Although ATmega328P execute code in 16 bit cells, when you read and write the flash memory, you actually have to use byte addresses in the Z register, and it is natural to use byte addresses to move data in or out the flash memory. Therefore, in 328eForth all flash addresses are byte addresses. Only when executing a command, its execution address in bytes is converted to a cell address. When you retrieve an address from flash memory or from the return stack, you have to convert it from a cell address to a byte address before operating on it.

4.2 Flash Programming

ATmega328P, with its Harvard architecture, is very hostile to FORTH. It is difficult to extend the FORTH system in flash memory. AmForth demonstrated that we can add new FORTH commands to the flash memory using a primitive command I!. However, it writes to flash memory one cell at a time, and this is very inefficient because it has to erase a page of flash memory and write the modified page back to flash. It could quickly exhaust the allowed erase-write cycles in the flash memory of ATmega328P.

The flash memory in ATmega328P is specified to endure 10,000 erase-write cycles. You have to be very careful about these erase-write cycles when you add new commands to the FORTH system. To minimize the erase-write cycles and to extend the life of flash memory, I took out the big gun in Chuck Moore's arsenal: the ping-pong BLOCK buffers.

I use two 128 byte page buffers in RAM to store compiled code. New FORTH commands are compiled into these buffers. Two buffers are necessary so that forward references can be resolved across a page boundary. Otherwise, many more erase-write cycles would be wasted when building structures in adjacent pages of flash memory. Only when both buffers are full, the least recently used buffer is flushed into the flash memory, before a new page of flash memory is read into this buffer.

The disadvantage is that after a new command is defined, you cannot execute it unless it is being flushed. Executing a command in a buffer will definitely crash the system. Always remember to include a FLUSH command at the end of a source code file. When you are compiling lines of code you type in, remember to do a FLUSH before executing any command you just typed in. Otherwise, be prepared to reload the system from AVR Studio 4. This error will happen, believe me, and it is disturbing. But, remember we are dealing with a microcontroller, and its flash memory can
endure only 10,000 erase-write cycles.

4.3 Number Formats

328eForth accepts only 16 bit numbers, positive, negative and prefixed. Number are accepted and converted according to a radix stored in variable BASE. The radix is set by the commands DECIMAL, HEX and BIN. Individual number may be prefixed by $ for hex. It will be converted without regard to BASE.

328eForth does not handle double integers in its number input and out put commands.

4.4 Memory Spaces

Fetch and store commands exist for the two address spaces (flash: I@, IC@, I!; and RAM: @, !, C@, C!). Parameters for constants are stored in flash, for variables and values, in RAM. The reason is to use slow to write flash for constants that are not changed, and variables and values in RAM that is fast to write. EEPROM memory is not used in 328eForth.

Care must be taken to know in which memory the allocation commands operate. These include

```
CREATE, DOES, ALLOT, IALLOT, :    ,    ',',
CMOVE,  DUMP, IDUMP, READ,   WRITE, and ERASE.
```

The top of each memory space is denoted by variables: CP for the flash dictionary, and DP for RAM. Note these are variables so their addresses are passed to the stack upon their execution.

Two pages of flash memory from $100-1FF are reserved to store initial values of variables and values. On boot-up, these two pages are copies to RAM at $100-1FF. When you want to build a turnkey system, this RAM area must be saved back to flash memory, so that next time the system boots up, new values are copied from flash to RAM.

Since flash memory is organized in 128 byte pages, commands operating on flash memory like IDUMP, READ, WRITE and ERASE all use page memory addresses and they operate on data in pages. DUMP also displays data in 128 byte pages, although it displays RAM memory.

There are DUMP command to view RAM memory and IDUMP command to view flash memory. They both accept a byte address and dump 128 bytes from the corresponding memory. 128 byte page is a convenient sized even for data in RAM memory.

4.5 Files

ATmega328P has only 2 KB of RAM memory, and it is not enough to handle files and other mass storage requirements. At present source files are sent to 328eForth for compiling through the serial terminal USB/COM port. To allow for interpretation and compilation, a pause must be inserted at the end of each line of text sent to 328eForth. I set the end of line delay in HyperTerminal to 900 ms. It probably could be half this value. Upon a compiling error an error message will be shown, but execution continues as the next lines of text are still streaming out of the serial port. You must manually watch for compilation errors. Generally, one error will cause many other errors, and 328eForth would crash if it tries to execute commands in the flash buffers. When this happens, reload 328eForth from AVR Studio 4.

4.6 Case Sensitivity

Both AmForth and eForth are case sensitive. AmForth uses lower case names and eForth uses upper case names. 328eForth is made case insensitive so that it can compile source code written for both AmForth and eForth. The command names in 328eForth are all in upper case, and commands typed in lower case are all converted to upper case before searching the dictionary. The names of new commands are all converted to upper case when they are compiled into dictionary in flash memory.

Case insensitive system is very friendly to you sitting in front of a terminal. However, you should also be careful in choosing names for commands so that they are not duplicated inadvertently.

4.7 What 328eForth Does Not Have

328eForth has no compiler security to check on the pairing of conditionals when compiling structures. Having an extra THEN in a colon definition will almost certainly blow the system up as it will write forward link randomly in earlier flash memory. In this case, execution will show odd errors; and you have to reload the 328eForth hex images. Do be careful when writing these structures:

```
IF...THEN
IF...ELSE...THEN
BEGIN...AGAIN
BEGIN...UNTIL
BEGIN...WHILE...REPEAT
FOR...NEXT
FOR...AFT...THEN...NEXT
```

Remember: Structures can be nested but cannot overlap.

328eForth does not support interrupts, multitasking, user variables, and local variables. However, the first 256 bytes of flash memory are reserved for interrupt vectors and for short interrupt service routines.

All commands in the 328eForth dictionary are linked in a single vocabulary. No multiple vocabularies.

328eForth does not have an assembler. If you have to code assembly routines, use AVR assembler in AVR Studio 4.

All these features can be added to 328eForth. But, it is better to keep it simple so people can understand if fully. If you have specific needs for specific tasks, I am sure you can somehow implement them or have people to help you.

ATmega328P is a small microcontroller. 328eForth is a seed we plant in it. You can make it to grow into something useful for you.

Chapter 5. 328eForth Source Code

ATmega328P is a very interesting microcontroller from Atmel Corp. It has an 8 bit CPU with 32 8 bit registers, 32 KB of flash memory, 2 KB of RAM memory, 1 KB of EEPROM memory, and a host of I/O devices. It is produced in a 28 pin DIP package, with 20 I/O pins. It is ideally suitable for many embedded applications. It is can be programmed to be a FORTH Virtual Machine.

The CPU registers are assigned various functions required in a FORTH Virtual Machine as follows:

Register	Alternate Name	Function
pc		Program counter
sp		Return stack pointer
r0		Reserved for multiply and memory operations
r1		Reserved for multiply and memory operations
r2	zerol	Provide constant 0
r3	zeroh	Provide constant 0
r4		Not used
r5		Not used
r6		Not used
r7		Not used
r8		Not used
r9		Not used
r10		Not used
r11		Not used
r12		Not used
r13		Not used

r14	temp4	Scratch pad
r15	temp5	Scratch pad
r16	temp0	Scratch pad
r17	temp1	Scratch pad
r18	temp2	Scratch pad
r19	temp3	Scratch pad
r20	temp6	Scratch pad
r21	temp7	Scratch pad
r22	looplo	Flash memory operations
r23	loophi	Flash memory operations
r24	tosl	Top of parameter stack low
r25	tosh	Top of parameter stack high
r26	xl	Scratch pad
r27	xh	Scratch pad
r28	yl	Parameter stack pointer low
r29	yh	Parameter stack pointer high
r30	zl	Used for memory address low
r31	zh	Used for memory address high

In 328eForth system, we adopt the Subroutine Threading Model, in which tokens are represented by subroutine call instructions, and a compound command consists of a list of subroutine call instructions. Nested token lists, as nested subroutine lists, are executed naturally by ATmega328P CPU with very little overhead in the nesting and un-nesting of subroutine calls and returns. It is also possible to mix tokens with CPU machine instructions when optimizing FORTH commands.

Using the Subroutine Threading Model, physically the compound commands has the identical structure as the primitive commands, and both types of commands are generally terminated by a ret machine instruction. However, in the assembly source listing, we still use the CODE macro to initialize a primitive command, and the COLON macro to initialize a compound command, although CODE and COLON macros are identical.

The CPU stack pointer register sp is used as the return stack pointer in the FORTH Virtual Machine, and the register pair yh ; yl is used as the parameter stack pointer. Both the return stack and the parameter stack are located in the high end of the RAM memory area. The top element of the parameter stack is cached in register pair tosh:tosl, and it significantly increases the speed in accessing the parameter stack.

The zh:zl register pair is used to address flash memory. The 4 register pairs tos, x, y, and z support many 16 bit operations, and make ATmega328P acting almost like a 16-bit CPU. They are used extensively in the primitive commands in 328eForth.

Besides the stacks, the RAM memory area also contains 16 system variable, the terminal input buffer, two buffers to access flash memory, areas for new variables and for input and output strings.

ATmega328P distinguishes two sections in its flash memory: a NRWW section in the high end of flash for bootloader, and a RWW section in the low end for application code. 328eForth puts its primitive commands and the interpreter in the bootloader section, because the interpreter must compile new compound commands in the application section of flash memory. As the 4KB space in the bootloader section is not big enough to host the entire 328eForth system, many compiler command are stored in the lower application section, which has space to add (compile) new compound commands.

A major advantage in using FORTH to develop software in microcontrollers is that we can interactively write and test small pieces of code on the target microcontroller. Writing and testing many small code fragments interactively necessitates writing and erasing flash memory, which will be problematic because flash memory have limited erasing cycles or life endurance. It is absolutely necessary to conserve flash memory erasing cycles. In 328eForth we use two 128-byte pages of RAM memory to store new code to minimize flash memory erasing cycles. Only when both buffers are full, the least used buffer is flushed to flash memory before it is used to access another page of flash memory.

In the original eForth Model, only 30 primitive commands were defined to enhance its portability to a wide range of microcontrollers. In the 328eForth implementation, to make it run as fast as possible, many compound commands are re-written in AVR assembly code, and all compound commands in the interpreter are coded using the relative call rcall and relative jump rjmp machine instructions, so that they can be squeezed into the 4 KB space in the bootloader section. The compound commands in the application section have to be coded using long call and long jmp instructions, because they have to call command in the bootloader section, which is outside of the range of rcall and rjmp machine instructions.

It is unfortunate that the 328eForth has to use the bootloader section to store its interpreter, and thus makes it incompatible with the Arduino bootloader. You have to make a choice to use one or the other. I hope that you will be convinced that 328eForth is a much better programming language and operating system for program development, and choose to use it in your future projects.

In the following sections, I will present the 328eForth system in its complete source listing. The source code is commented liberally. However, in-line comments are only adequate to document the functions of the source code, but not sufficient for the intentions behind the source code. To give myself enough room to discuss the structures and the design requirements of all the commands, for one section of source code, I add another section for comments. I hope this format will let me explain more fully what the commands do and what was intended for them to do.

```
; TITLE Atmega328 eForth
.nolist
 .include "m328Pdef.inc"
.list
;===================================================
; 328eForth v3.01, Chen-Hanson Ting, July 2011
;  Fix error, quit, 2/ and ?stack
;
; 328eForth v2.10, Chen-Hanson Ting, March 2011
; Adapted from
;  86se4th.asm by Richard Haskell
;  Amforth by Matthias Trute
; Assembled with AVR Studio 4 from Atmel
; -Subroutine threaded model
; -Uniform byte addressing for flash, RAM and
;  registers
; -Ping-pong block buffers for optimal flash
;  programming
; -FORTH interpreter & tools are in NRWW flash
; -FORTH compiler & user extension are
;  in RWW flash
; -No interrupt, no multitasking
; -turnkey capability
; -Case insensitive
; -9600 baud, 1 start, 8 data, no parity, 1 stop bit ;
; ANS FORTH compatible, but not compliant.
;
; Subroutine threaded eForth; Version. 1.0, 1991
; by Richard E. Haskell
; Dept. of Computer Science and Engineering
; Oakland University
; Rochester, Michigan 48309
;
; eForth 1.0 by Bill Muench and C. H. Ting, 1990
; Much of the code is derived from the
;  following sources:
; 8086 figForth by Thomas Newman,
; 1981 and Joe Smith, 1983
```

```
; aFORTH by John Rible
; bFORTH by Bill Muench


; The goal of this implementation is to provide a
; simple eForth Model which can be ported easily
```

```
; to many  8, 16, 24 and 32 bit CPU's.
; You are invited to implement this Model on your
; favorite CPU and contribute it to the eForth Library
; for public use.
; You may use a portable implementation to advertise
; more sophisticated and optimized versions for
; commercial purposes.
; However, you are expected to implement the Model
; faithfully.
; The eForth Working Group reserves the right to
; reject implementations which deviates significantly
; from this  Model.
;
; Representing the eForth Working Group in the
; Silicon Valley FIG Chapter
; Send contributions to:

; Dr. Chen-Hanson Ting
; 156 14th Avenue
; San Mateo, CA 94402
; (650) 571-7639
; ting@offete.com
```

5.1 FORTH Virtual Machine on ATmega328P

328Pdef.inc contains all the register names and names of bits in these registers. It is included here first so that we can refer to the registers and bits with mnemonic names.

In the original eForth Model, a small group of FORTH commands were identified as kernel commands, low level commands, or primitive commands. These commands were coded in machine instructions of the host microprocessor. They allow the underlying microcontroller to become a FORTH Virtual Machine. All other commands were written as lists of commands, and are called high level commands or compound commands. Compound commands are lists of primitive commands and other compound commands. This division of commands was very useful in porting eForth to many different microprocessors, because only primitive commands needed to be rewritten when moving eForth to a new microprocessor.

In 328eForth, we retained this division. However, we use the Subroutine Threading Model and optimize many compound commands so that the system executes at the highest speed and occupies the least memory space. All commands that can be optimized are re-coded in assembly.

ATmega328P addresses RAM memory in bytes, but addresses flash memory in 16-bit cells. Two different addressing mechanisms make it difficult to move data between these two memory areas. After agonizing over this difference for some time, I decided to address all memories in bytes. When you try to read and write the flash memory, you will find that you have to read and write it in bytes. We might just as well use byte addresses to access flash memory. A byte address is converted to a cell address which you have to jump to locations in flash, or to execute code in flash.

Two 128-byte buffers are allocated in RAM to hold data to be written into flash memory. These buffers minimize erasing cycles of flash memory.

The original eForth Model is case sensitive. 328eForth is made case insensitive by converting all input characters to upper case, and all command names are stored as upper case characters. This is very useful in compiling applications from different sources, where FORTH commands might be in upper, lower, or mixed cases.

The only I/O device required by 328eForth system is a serial UART device operating at 19,200 baud, 1 start bit, 8 data bits, not parity, 1 stop bit, and no flow control. Since in ATmega328P, all I/O registers are mapped into the first 256 bytes in the RAM space, we can conveniently control all its I/O devices by C! and C@ commands.

328eForth is intended to be used by first time FORTH users. Interrupts and multitasking are not supported. Nevertheless, provisions are put in so that sophisticate users can add interrupts. The first 256 bytes in the flash memory is reserved for reset and interrupt vector table. The next 256 bytes in the flash memory are used to store initial values allocated to RAM memory locations $100-$1FF. Therefore, you can build a turn-key application in ATmega328P with 328eForth system.

```
;; Version control

.EQU VER = 2 ;major release version
.EQU EXT = 2 ;minor extension

;; Constants

.EQU COMPO = $040 ;lexicon compile only bit
.EQU IMEDD = $080 ;lexicon immediate bit
.EQU BASEE = 16  ;default radix
.EQU BKSPP = 8  ;back space
.EQU LF  = 10  ;line feed
.EQU CRR  = 13  ;carriage return
.EQU RETT = $9508
.EQU CALLL = $940E

;; Memory allocation for ATmega328P, all byte
;  addresses
;
; Flash memory
; $0  Reset and interrupt vectors, RWW section
; $100 Initial values for variables
; $200 Start of compiler and user words
; $7000 Start of interpreter words, NRWW section
; $7FFF End of flash memory
;
; RAM memory
; $0  CPU and I/O registers
; $100 Variables
; $120 Free RAM memory
; $160 Initial PAD
; $6F0 Top of data stack
; $700 Terminal input buffer
; $7F0 Top of return stack
; $800 Flash buffer 0
; $880 Flash buffer 1
; $8FF End of RAM memory

.EQU RPP  = $7F0 ;start of return stack (RP0)
.EQU TIBB = $700 ;terminal input buffer (TIB)
.EQU UPP  = $100 ;start of user area (UP0)
.EQU SPP  = $6F0 ;start of data stack (SP0)
```

```
;; Flash programmming

.EQU BUF0 = $800
.EQU BUF1 = $880
.EQU NEWER = $11C ;flash pointer
.EQU OLDER = $11E ;flash pointer
; buffer pointer word format:
; dirty,page_addr,cell_addr,buf?
```

5.1.1 Constants Used by Assembler

Constant	Value	Function
VER	2	Major release version
EXT	2	Minor extension
COMPO	$40	Lexicon compile-only bit
IMEDD	$80	Lexicon immediate bit
BASEE	16	Default radix for number conversion
BKSPP	8	Back space ASCII character
LF	10	Line feed ASCII character
CRR	13	Carriage return ASCII character
RETT	$9508	Machine code of ret instruction
CALLL	$940E	Machine code of call instruction
RPP	$7F0	Top of return stack (RP0)
TIBB	$700	Terminal input buffer (TIB)
UPP	$100	Start of user area (UP0)
SPP	$6F0	Top of parameter stack (SP0)
BUF0	$800	Address of first flash buffer
BUF1	$880	Address if second flash buffer
NEWER	$11C	Pointer to the NEW buffer
OLDER	$11E	Pointer to the OLD buffer

Flash Memory Allocation of 328eForth in Bytes

Address	Contents
$0	Reset and interrupt vectors, RWW section
$100	Initial values for variables
$200	Start of compiler and user commands
$7000	Start of interpreter commands, NRWW section
$7FFF	End of flash memory

RAM Memory Allocation of 328eForth in Bytes

Address	Contents
$0	CPU and I/O registers
$100	Variables
$120	Free RAM memory
$160	Initial PAD for number conversions
$6F0	Top of parameter stack
$700	Terminal input buffer
$7F0	Top of return stack
$800	Flash buffer 0
$880	Flash buffer 1
$8FF	End of RAM memory

```
;; Initialize assembly variable

.SET _LINK  = 0  ;init a null link

; Compile a code definition header.

.MACRO CODE    ;;LEX,NAME
 .DW  _LINK*2  ;;link pointer
 .SET _LINK = pc  ;;link points to a name string
 .DB  @0,@1
```

```
.ENDM

; Colon header is identical to code header.

.MACRO COLON   ;;LEX,NAME,LABEL
.DW  _LINK*2  ;;link pointer
.SET _LINK = pc  ;;link points to a name string
.DB  @0,@1
.ENDM
```

5.1.2 Headers

_LINK is an assembly variable which stored the name field address in the header of the prior command. It is initialize to 0, to signify that the first command is at the end of the linked list of command records.

CODE is an assembly macro to build headers for primitive commands in the 328eForth system. It is used in the following fashion:

```
CODE 4,"EMIT"
```

It expects two arguments: a one byte number and a byte string.

CODE macro first allocates two bytes for a link field, and places the contents in _LINK into this link field. Then, _LINK is updated to point to the next location as stored in a system variable pc. Next, it assembles two arguments in its DB statement, which builds up the name field of the command.

CODE macro builds the header of a primitive command. Following this header, the assembly will assemble ATmega328P machine instructions to fill the code field of this FORTH primitive command.

COLON builds the header of a compound command. It is exactly the same as CODE, because we are using the Subroutine Threading Model, and the token list in the code field of a compound command consists of a list of call instructions, which are machine instructions of ATmega328P.

The following figure shows the structures of primitive and compound commands.

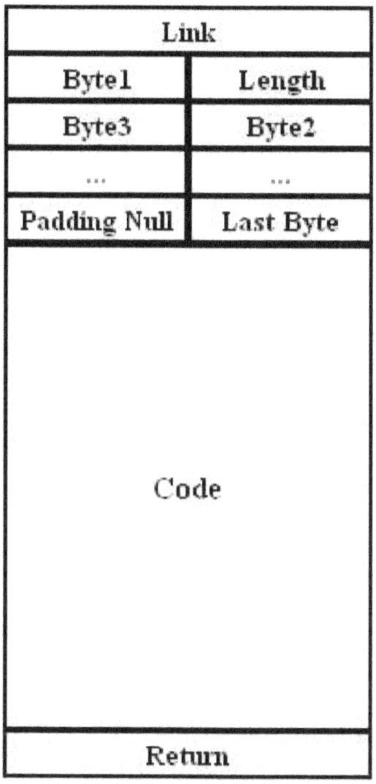

Primitive Command

Compound Command

```
;; Macros defined by amForth

.DEF zerol = r2
.DEF zeroh = r3
.DEF temp4 = r14
.DEF temp5 = r15
.DEF temp0 = r16
.DEF temp1 = r17
.DEF temp2 = r18
.DEF temp3 = r19
.DEF temp6 = r20
.DEF temp7 = r21
```

```
.DEF tosl = r24
.DEF tosh = r25

.macro loadtos  ld tosl, Y+  ld tosh, Y+
.endmacro

.macro savetos  st -Y, tosh  st -Y, tosl
.endmacro

.macro in_ .if (@1 < $40)    in @0,@1 .else
 lds @0,@1
.endif
.endmacro

.macro out_ .if (@0 < $40)    out @0,@1
.else    sts @0,@1
.endif
.endmacro

.macro readflashcell  lsl zl  rol zh
 lpm @0, Z+  lpm @1, Z+
.endmacro
```


```
.DEF tosl = r24
.DEF tosh = r25

.macro loadtos  ld tosl, Y+  ld tosh, Y+
.endmacro

.macro savetos  st -Y, tosh  st -Y, tosl
.endmacro

.macro in_ .if (@1 < $40)    in @0,@1 .else
 lds @0,@1
.endif
.endmacro

.macro out_ .if (@0 < $40)    out @0,@1
.else    sts @0,@1
.endif
.endmacro
```

```
.macro readflashcell lsl zl rol zh
lpm @0, Z+ lpm @1, Z+
.endmacro
```

5.1.3 Assembly Macros

The most important register names are defined in 328pdef.inc provided by Atmel. Among them yh:yl pair is used as parameter stack pointer, and zh:zl pair is used to address flash memory. xh:xl pair can be used freely, and in many cases are used to hold the second item on the parameter stack, which are used with the top item on parameter stack, but cached in tosh:tosl register pair.

LOADTOS	Pop the external parameter stack and copy the popped item into tosh:tosl register pair. It is used to implement DROP commands, and many other commands consuming the top two items on the parameter stack. It uses yh;yl register pair in post-increment addressing mode
SAVETOS	Push the top item on the parameter stack, which is cached in tosh:tosl register pair, on the external parameter stack. It is used to implement DUP command, and commands which pushes new data on the parameter stack. It uses yh:yl register pair in the pre-decrement addressing mode.
IN_	Read data from an input register. It examines the register address. For a normal input register, it assembles an in instruction. For an extended input register, it assembles a lds instruction.
OUT_	Write data to an output register. It examines the register address. For a normal output register, it assembles an out instruction. For an extended input register, it assembles a sts instruction.

READFLAS HCELL	Assume that zh:zl register pair contains a cell address pointing to a location in flash memory. As the flash memory must be addressed in bytes, this cell address is shifted left by 1 bit, and two consecutive bytes from flash memory are read into a pair of destination register. This macro reveals the fact that flash memory in ATmega328P is actually organized in bytes. Consequently, I organized 328eForth using byte addresses to access both RAM and flash memory. It is astatically much more pleasing than using different addressing schemes for different types of memory.

in_ and out_ macros take care of the strange I/O architecture in ATmega328P chip. In the original design only 64 I/O registers were allocated, and uses in and out instructions to access them. The I/O space is much too small, and had to be extended to encompass 256 registers.

5.1.4 Variables and Startup Code

Flash memory location 0-$FF is allocated for a reset vector, interrupt vector table and interrupt service routines. The reset vector at location 0 contains an address pointing to the reset routine START.

Flash memory location $100-1FF, cell address $80-FF, are reserved to store initial values of variables in the RAM memory starting at RAM location $100. After 328eForth boots up, it copies 256 bytes from a flash memory array starting at $100 to RAM memory array starting at $100. This way you can build a turn-key system with your application.

```
;; Main entry points and COLD start data

 .CSEG
 .ORG 0
 JMP  START

 .ORG $80  ;byte address $100,
    ;copy to ram on boot,
    ;saved from ram for turnkey system

UZERO:
 .DW  HI*2 ;'BOOT
 .DW  0  ;reserved
 .DW  BASEE ;BASE
 .DW  0  ;tmp
 .DW  0  ;SPAN  .DW  0  ;>IN
 .DW  0  ;#TIB
 .DW  TIBB ;TIB
```

```
 .DW  INTER*2 ;'EVAL
 .DW  0  ;HLD
 .DW  LASTN ;CONTEXT pointer
 .DW  CTOP ;CP
 .DW  DTOP ;DP
 .DW  LASTN ;LAST
 .DW  $6F00 ;PTR0 to BUF0
 .DW  $6F81 ;PTR1 to BUF1
ULAST:

 .ORG $3800
;byte address $7000
START:
 in_  r10, MCUSR  clr  r11  clr  zerol  clr
 zeroh  out_  MCUSR, zerol
; init return stack pointer
ldi  xl,low(RPP)  out_  SPL,xl
ldi  xh,high(RPP)
out_  SPH,xh
; init parameter stack pointer
ldi  yl,low(SPP)  ldi  yh,high(SPP)
; jump to Forth starting word
jmp  COLD
```

The first 32 bytes starting at location $100 are used by system variables, as shown in the following list:

Variable	Address	Function
'BOOT	100	Execution vector to start application command.
	102	Reserved
BASE	104	Radix base for numeric conversion.
tmp	106	Scratch pad.
HLD	108	Pointer to a buffer holding next digit for numeric conversion.
SPAN	10A	Number of characters received by EXPECT.
>IN	10C	Input buffer character pointer used by text interpreter.
#TIB	10E	Number of characters in input buffer.
'TIB	110	Address of Terminal Input Buffer.
'EVAL	112	Execution vector switching between $INTERPRET and $COMPILE.
CONTEXT	114	Vocabulary array pointing to last name fields of dictionary.
CP	116	Pointer to top of dictionary, the first available flash memory location to compile new command
DP	118	Pointer to the first available RAM memory location.
LAST	11A	Pointer to name field of last command in dictionary.
NEW	11C	Pointer to most recently used flash memory buffer.
OLD	11E	Pointer to the flash memory buffer not used recently, to
		be flushed back to flash memory

The startup routine START is located at the beginning of the bootloader section in flash memory, at location $7000 (cell address $3800). It first clears registers zerol, zeroh, and the CPU status register MCUSR. It then initializes the return stack pointer in the SP register, and the parameter stack pointer in yh:yl register pair. It thus completes hardware initialization, and then jumps to COLD command which initializes the 328eForth FORTH Virtual Machine, and starts running an application. The default application in 328eForth is HI, which simply sends out a sign-on message and falls into the text interpreter QUIT. The address of HI is stored in memory location named 'BOOT at $100 (both in flash and in RAM memory). This address can be changed to point to an application command in a turnkey system.

5.1.5 Device Dependent I/O

The only I/O device used by 328eForth system is the serial communication device USART0 in ATmega328P chip.

```
;; Device dependent I/O

; ?RX ( -- c T | F )
; Return input character and true,
; or a false if no input.

 CODE 4,"?KEY"
QRX:
QKEY:
 savetos clr tosl clr tosh
 movw tosl,zerol
 in_ xl,UCSR0A sbrs xl,7
 ret
 in_ tosl,UDR0
 savetos ser tosl ser tosh
 ret

; TX! ( c -- )
; Send character c to the output device.

 CODE 4,"EMIT"
EMIT:
TXSTO:
 in_ xl,UCSR0A sbrs xl,5 rJMP TXSTO
```

```
out_ UDR0,tosl
load tos
ret

; !IO ( -- )
; Initialize the serial I/O devices.

; CODE 3,"!IO"
STOIO:
ldi xl,$66 ;19200 baud out_ UBRR0L,xl
clr xl out_ UBRR0H,xl
ldi xl,$18 ;enable TX and RX out_
UCSR0B,xl ldi xl,6 ;8 data bits
out_ UCSR0C,xl
RET
```

!IO	Initialize USART0 device. It writes $66 into baud rate register pair UBRR0H:UBRR0L to set up the baud rate to 9600 baud. It writes $18 into control register UCSR0B to enable both transmitter and receiver in USART0. It then write $6 into control register UCSR0C to set up the data format to 1 start bit, 8 data bits, no parity, 1 stop bit, and no flow control.
?KEY	Examine the status register UCSR0A to see if there is a valid character in the receiver. If a character is received, ?KEY reads the ASCII code of the character in data register UDR0 and pushes it on the parameter stack. It then pushes a true flag on the top. If no character is received, it only pushes a false flag on the parameter stack.
EMIT	Send a character to the transmitter. It first waits on the transmitter buffer empty flag in UCSR0A register. When the transmitter is ready to transmit, it pops the character off the parameter stack and writes it into the transmitter data register UDR0.

5.1.6 Kernel

doLIT command is used to build literal structures in compound commands. It allows numbers to be pushed on the parameter stack when the compound command is executed.

```
;; The kernel

;   doLIT ( w -- )
; Push an inline literal.

; CODE COMPO+5,"doLIT" DOLIT:
 savetos  pop  zh  pop  zl
 readflashcell tosl,tosh
 ror  zh  ror  zl  push zl
 push zh  ret
```

```
;   next ( -- )
; Run time code for the single index loop.

; CODE COMPO+4,"next" DONXT:
 POP  zh ;ret addr
 POP  zl ;  pop  xh ;count
 pop  xl  sbiw xl, 1
 brge NEXT1  adiw zl,1
 push zl  push zh  ret
NEXT1:
 push xl ;push count back  push xh
 readflashcell xl,xh  push xl  push xh  ret
```

next	Build indexed loop structures in compound command. A loop starts when the loop index is pushed on the return stack. When it is executed, it decrements this loop index on the return stack. If resulting index is not negative, jump back to repeat the loop. If the resulting index is negative, pop the return stack to discard the index, and exit the loop.

The literal structure and the indexed loop structure are show in the following figure:

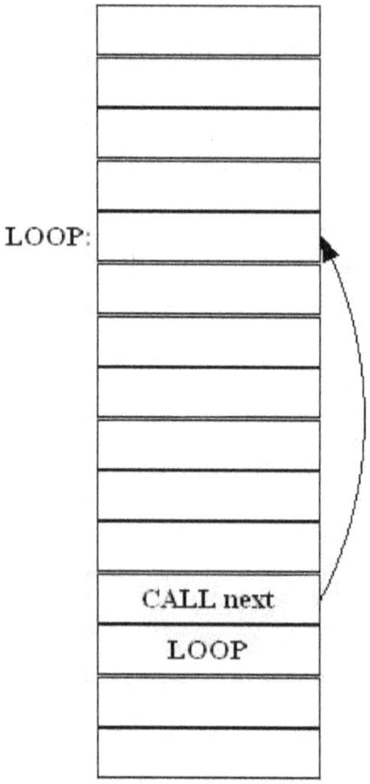

Loop Structure

Literal Structure

5.1.7 Flow Control

?branch and branch commands are used to build control structures and loop structures in compound commands. In the following figure, an IF-ELSE-THEN branch structure and a BEGIN-WHILE-REPEAT loop structure are illustrated:

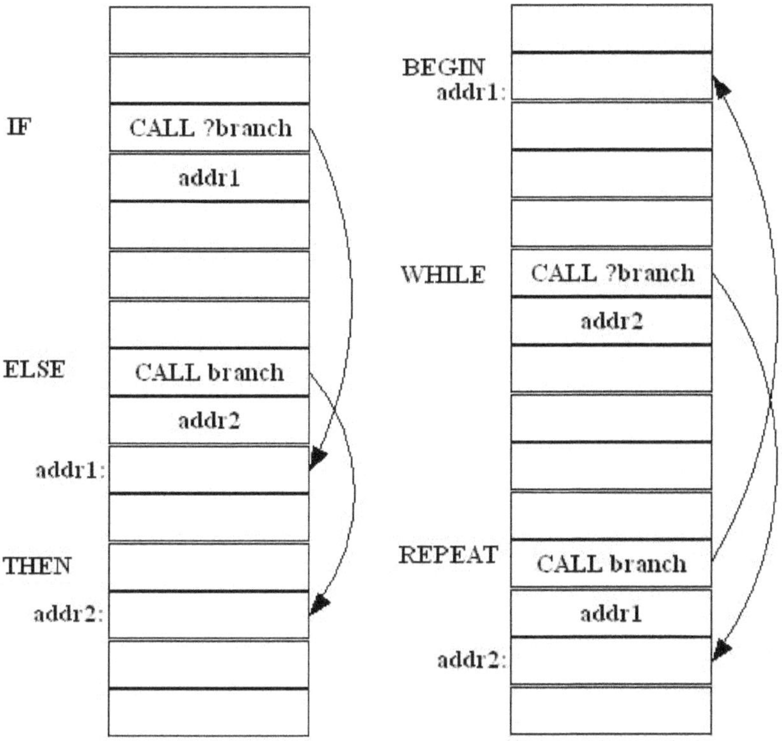

IF-ELSE-THEN
Branch Structure

BEGIN-WHILE-REPEAT
Loop Structure

```
;   ?branch ( f -- )
; Branch if flag is zero.

; CODE COMPO+7,"?branch" QBRAN:
 pop  zh  pop  zl  or  tosl, tosh  loadtos
 breq BRAN1  adiw zl,1  push zl
 push zh
 ret

;   branch ( -- )
; Branch to an inline address.

; CODE COMPO+6,"branch" BRAN:
 pop  zh  pop  zl
```

```
BRAN1:
 readflashcell xl,xh
 push xl
 push xh
 ret

;  EXECUTE ( b -- )
; Execute the word at ca=b/2.

 CODE 7,"EXECUTE"
EXECU:
 asr tosh ;b/2 ror tosl
 push tosl  push tosh
 loadtos  ret

;  EXIT ( -- )
; Terminate current colon word.

 CODE 4,"EXIT"
EXIT:
 pop xh pop xl ret
```

?branch	Build a conditional branch in compound commands.
branch	Build an unconditional branch in compound commands.
EXECUTE	Jump to an execution address on the top of the parameter stack. As the execution address is a byte address, it must be converted to a cell address for jumping. The cell address is pushed on the return stack and a RET instruction is executed to cause the jump.
EXIT	Terminate a compound command. Since it is executed as a call EXIT command, the return address must be popped off the return stack and then a ret instruction is executed. It is retained for compatibility. The call EXIT command can be simply replaced by a ret machine instruction.

5.1.8 RAM Memory Access

ATmega328P has separated RAM memory and flash memory. Two different memories need two separate sets of command to read and write them.

```
; !(wa--)
; Pop the data stack to memory.

 CODE 1,"!"
STORE:
 movw zl, tosl loadtos std Z+1,
 tosh std Z+0, tosl
 loadtos
 RET

; @ ( a -- w )
; Push memory location to the data stack.

 CODE 1,"@"
AT:
 movw zl, tosl ld  tosl, z+ ld  tosh, z+
 RET

; C! ( c b -- )
; Pop the data stack to byte memory.

 CODE 2,"C!"
CSTOR:
 movw zl, tosl loadtos st  Z, tosl loadtos
 RET

; C@ ( b -- c )
; Push byte memory location to the data stack.

 CODE 2,"C@"
CAT:
 movw zl, tosl clr tosh ld  tosl, Z
 RET
```

@	Read a 16-bit data stored in the address on top of the parameter stack. The address is a byte address pointing to a location in RAM meory.
!	Store the 16-bit data as the second item on parameter stack into the address on top of the parameter stack.
C@	Read an 8-bit data stored in the address on top of the parameter stack.
C!	Store an 8-bit data as the second item on parameter stack into the address on top of the parameter stack.

These 4 memory commands access data stored in RAM memory. Since in ATmega328P, the CPU registers and I/O registers are mapped to the RAM memory space from 0 to $FF, we can control ATmega328P interactively using these commands. This is the greatest advantage 328eForth has over the Arduino operating system which is a Compile-Load-Test no-interactive system.

To access flash memory, we have the corresponding I@, I!, and IC@ commands. They are discussed in a later section.

5.1.9 Return Stack

328eForth system uses the return stack for two specific purposes: to save addresses while recursing through a token list, and to store the loop index for a FOR-NEXT loop.

Return stack is used by the FORTH Virtual Machine to save return addresses to be processed later. It is also a convenient place to store data temporarily. The return stack can thus be considered as an extension of the parameter stack. However, one must be very careful in using the return stack for temporary storage. The data pushed on the return stack must be popped off before ret is executed. Otherwise, ret will get the wrong address to return to, and the system generally will crash. Since >R and R> are very dangerous to use, they are designed as compile-only commands and you can only use them in the compiling mode.

In setting up a loop, FOR compiles >R, which pushes the loop index from the parameter stack to the return stack. Inside the FOR-NEXT loop, the running index can be recalled by R@. NEXT compiles call next with an address after FOR. when next is executed, it decrements the loop index on the top of the return stack. If the index becomes negative, the loop is terminated; otherwise, next jumps back to the command after FOR.

```
;  R> ( -- w )
; Pop the return stack to the data stack.

 CODE COMPO+2,"R>"
RFROM:
 savetos pop xh pop xl pop tosh
 pop tosl push xl push xh
 RET

;  R@ ( -- w )
; Copy top of return stack to the data stack.

 CODE 2,"R@"
RAT:
 savetos pop xh pop xl pop tosh
 pop tosl push tosl push tosh push xl
 push xh
 RET

;  >R ( w -- )
; Push the data stack to the return stack.

 CODE COMPO+2,">R"
TOR:
 pop xh
 pop xl
 push tosl
 push tosh
 push xl
 loadtos
 RET
```

>R	Pop a number off the parameter stack and pushes it on the return stack.
R>	Pop a number off the return stack and pushes it on the parameter stack.

R@	Copy the top item on the return stack and pushes it on the parameter stack without disturbing the return stack

5.1.10 Parameter Stack

The parameter stack is the central location where all numerical data are processed, and where parameters are passed from one command to another. The stack items have to be arranged properly so that they can be retrieved in the Last-In-First-Out (LIFO) manner. When stack items are out of order, they can be rearranged by the stack words DUP, SWAP, OVER and DROP. There are other stack words useful in manipulating stack items, but these four are considered to be the minimum set.

```
;   SP@ ( -- a )
; Push the current data stack pointer.

; CODE 3,"SP@"
SPAT:
 savetos  movw tosl, yl
 RET

;   SP! ( a -- )
; Set the data stack pointer.

; CODE 3,"SP!"
SPSTO:
 movw  yl, tosl  loadtos
 RET

;   DROP ( w -- )
; Discard top stack item.

 CODE 4,"DROP"
DROP:
 loadtos
 RET

;   DUP ( w -- w w )
; Duplicate the top stack item.

 CODE 3,"DUP"
```

```
DUPP:
 savetos
 RET

;  SWAP ( w1 w2 -- w2 w1 )
; Exchange top two stack items.

 CODE 4,"SWAP"
SWAPP:
 movw  xl, tosl  ld  tosl,Y+  ld  tosh,Y+
 st   -Y, xh  st   -Y, xl
 RET

;  OVER ( w1 w2 -- w1 w2 w1 )
; Copy second stack item to top.

 CODE 4,"OVER"
OVER:
 savetos  ldd  tosl, Y+2  ldd  tosh, Y+3
 RET
```

SP!	Initialize the parameter stack.
SP@	Return the depth of parameter stack.
DROP	Pop the parameter stack discards the top item on it.
DUP	Duplicate the top item and pushes it on the parameter stack.
SWAP	Exchange the two two item on the parameter stack.
OVER	Duplicates the second item and pushes it on the parameter stack.

5.1.11 Logic

The only primitive command which cares about logic is ?branch. It tests the top item on the stack. If it is zero, ?branch will branch to the following address. If it is not zero, ?branch will ignore the address and execute the command after the branch address. Thus we distinguish two logic values, zero for false and non-zero for true. Numbers used this way are called logic flags which can be either true or false. Logic flags thus cause conditional branching in control structures.

```
; 0< ( n -- t )
; Return true if n is negative.

 CODE 2,"0<"
ZLESS:
 tst tosh
 movw tosl, zerol brge ZLESS1 sbiw tosl,1
ZLESS1:
RET
```

```
; AND ( w w -- w )
; Bitwise AND.

 CODE 3,"AND"
ANDD:
 ld xl, Y+ ld xh, Y+ and tosl, xl
 and tosh, xh
 RET

; OR ( w w -- w )
; Bitwise inclusive OR.

 CODE 2,"OR"
ORR:
 ld xl, Y+ ld xh, Y+ or tosl,
 xl or tosh, xh
 RET

; XOR ( w w -- w )
; Bitwise exclusive OR.
```

```
CODE 3,"XOR"
XORR:
ld  xl, Y+ ld  xh, Y+
  eor  tosl, xl eor  tosh, xh
RET

;  UM+ ( u u -- udsum )
; Add two unsigned single numbers
; and return a double sum.

CODE 3,"UM+"
UPLUS:
ld  xl, Y+ ld  xh, Y+ add  tosl,
xl adc  tosh, xh  savetos clr  tosh
clr  tosl  rol  tosl
RET
```

0<	Examine the top item on the parameter stack for its negativeness. If it is negative, 0< will return a -1 for true. If it is 0 or positive, 0< will return a 0 for false.
AND	Remove top two items on the parameter stack and pushes their bitwise logic AND results on the parameter stack.
OR	Remove top two items on the parameter stack and pushes their bitwise
	logic OR results on the parameter stack.
XOR	Remove top two items on the parameter stack and pushes their bitwise logic exclusive OR results on the parameter stack.
UM+	Add top two unsigned number on the data stack and replaces them with the unsigned sum of these two numbers and a carry on top of the sum. FORTH does not have access to the carry flag in ATmega328P CPU, and UM+ preserves the carry flag to be used in double integer arithmetic operations. In 328eForth, most arithmetic commands are coded in assembly and UM+ is not used often.

5.1.12 System Variables

In 328eForth, all variables used by the system are merged together and are called system variables. They are allocated in a RAM memory array starting from location $100. They are all initialized by copying a table of initial values stored in flash memory starting from location $100.

```
;; System and user variables

;  doVAR ( -- a )
; Run time routine for VARIABLE and CREATE.

; CODE COMPO+5,"doVAR" DOVAR:
 savetos  pop  zh  pop  zl
 readflashcell tosl,tosh
 RET

;  'BOOT ( -- a )
; Storage of application address.

 COLON 5,"'BOOT"
TBOOT:
 RCALL DOVAR
 .DW  UPP

;  BASE ( -- a )
; Storage of the radix base for numeric I/O.

 COLON 4,"BASE"
BASE:
 RCALL DOVAR
 .DW  UPP+4

;  tmp ( -- a )
; A temporary storage location used in
; parse and find.

 COLON 3,"TMP"
TEMP:
 RCALL DOVAR
 .DW  UPP+6
```

```
;   SPAN ( -- a )
; Hold character count received by EXPECT.

 COLON 4,"SPAN"
SPAN:
 RCALL DOVAR
 .DW  UPP+8

;   >IN ( -- a )
; Hold the character pointer while parsing
; input stream.

 COLON 3,">IN"
INN:
 RCALL DOVAR
 .DW  UPP+10

;   #TIB ( -- a )
; Hold the current count in and address
; of the terminal input buffer.

 COLON 4,"#TIB"
NTIB:
 RCALL DOVAR
 .DW  UPP+12

;   'TIB ( -- a )
; Hold the current count in and address
; of the terminal input buffer.

 COLON 4,"'TIB"
TTIB:
 RCALL DOVAR
 .DW  UPP+14

;   'EVAL ( -- a )
; Execution vector of EVAL.

 COLON 5,"'EVAL"
TEVAL:
 RCALL DOVAR
```

```
 .DW  UPP+16

;  HLD ( -- a )
; Hold a pointer in building a numeric
; output string.

 COLON 3,"HLD"
HLD:
 RCALL DOVAR
 .DW  UPP+18

;  CONTEXT ( -- a )
; A area to specify vocabulary search order.

 COLON 7,"CONTEXT" CNTXT:
 RCALL DOVAR
 .DW  UPP+20

;  CP ( -- a )
; Point to the top of the code dictionary.
```

```
 COLON 2,"CP"
CPP:
 RCALL DOVAR
 .DW  UPP+22

;  DP ( -- a )
; Point to the free RAM space.
 COLON 2,"DP"
DPP:
 RCALL DOVAR
 .DW  UPP+24

;  LAST ( -- a )
; Point to the last name in the name dictionary.

 COLON 4,"LAST"
LAST:
 RCALL DOVAR
 .DW  UPP+26
```

doVAR	Fetch a value stored after the call doVAR instruction and pushes it on the parameter stack. It returns to its caller immediately. call doVAR instruction and the value after it forms the code field in all variable commands, with the value pointing to a location in RAM memory.

Variable	Address	Function
'BOOT	100	Execution vector to start application command.
	102	Reserved
BASE	104	Radix base for numeric conversion.
tmp	106	Scratch pad.
HLD	108	Pointer to a buffer holding next digit for numeric conversion.
SPAN	10A	Number of characters received by EXPECT.
>IN	10C	Input buffer character pointer used by text interpreter.
#TIB	10E	Number of characters in input buffer.
'TIB	110	Address of Terminal Input Buffer.
'EVAL	112	Execution vector switching between $INTERPRET and $COMPILE.
CONTEXT	114	Vocabulary array pointing to last name fields of dictionary.
CP	116	Pointer to top of dictionary, the first available flash memory location to compile new command
DP	118	Pointer to the first available RAM memory location.
LAST	11A	Pointer to name field of last command in dictionary.

NEW	11C	Pointer to most recently used flash memory buffer.
OLD	11E	Pointer to the flash memory buffer not used recently, to be flushed back to flash memory

5.2 Common Functions

5.2.1 Arithmetic

This group of FORTH commands are commonly used in writing FORTH applications. In the original eForth Model they are coded as compound commands to enhance the portability of eForth. Here in 328eForth implementations, they are coded in assembly language to increase the execute speed.

```
;; Common functions

;  2* ( n -- n )
; Multiply tos by cell size in bytes.

 COLON 2,"2*"
CELLS:
 lsl  tosl  rol  tosh  ret

;  2/ ( n -- n )
; Divide tos by cell size in bytes.

 COLON 2,"2/"
TWOSL:
 asr  tosh  ror  tosl  ret

;  ALIGNED ( b -- a )
; Align address to the cell boundary.

; COLON 7,"ALIGNED" ALGND:
 adiw tosl,1  andi tosl,254  ret

;  BL ( -- 32 )
```

```
; Return 32, the blank character.

 COLON 2,"BL"
BLANK:
 savetos ldi tosl,32 clr tosh ret

;  ?DUP ( w -- w w | 0 )
; Dup tos if its is not zero.

 COLON 4,"?DUP"
QDUP:   mov temp0, tosl   or  temp0, tosh   breq QDUP1   savetos
QDUP1:
 RET
```

2*	Shift the top item on the parameter stack left by 1 bit. Multiply by 2.
2/	Shift the top item on the parameter stack right by 1 bit. Divide by 2.
ALIGNED	Modify the byte address on top of the parameter stack so that it points to the next word boundary.
BL	Push a blank or space character (ASCII 32) on parameter stack. BL is often used in parsing out space delimited strings.
?DUP	Duplicate the top item on the parameter stack if it is non-zero.

```
;  ROT ( w1 w2 w3 -- w2 w3 w1 ) ; Rot 3rd
                        ;item to top.

 COLON 3,"ROT"
ROT:
   movw  temp0, tosl    ld  temp2, Y+
   ld  temp3, Y+
   loadtos    st  -Y, temp3  st  -Y, temp2
   st  -Y, temp1    st  -Y, temp0
 RET
```

```
;  2DROP ( w w -- )
; Discard two items on stack.

 COLON 5,"2DROP"
DDROP:
 loadtos  loadtos  ret

;  2DUP ( w1 w2 -- w1 w2 w1 w2 )
; Duplicate top two items.

 COLON 4,"2DUP"
DDUP:
 RCALL OVER  RJMP OVER

;  + ( w w -- sum )
; Add top two items.

 COLON 1,"+"
PLUS:
  ld  temp0, Y+    ld  temp1, Y+
. add  tosl, temp0    adc  tosh, temp1
 RET
```

```
;  NOT ( w -- w )
; One's complement of tos.

 COLON 6,"INVERT"
INVER:
   com  tosl    com  tosh
 ret
```

ROT	Rotate the top three items on the parameter stack. The third item is pulled out to the top. The second item is pushed down to the third item, and the top item is pushed down to be the second item. ROT is unique in that it accesses the third item on the parameter stack. All other stack commands can only access one or two stack items. In FORTH programming, it is generally accepted that one should not try to access stack items deeper than the third item. When you have to access deeper into the data stack, it is a good time to re-evaluate

	your algorithm. Most often, you can avoid this situation by factoring your code into smaller parts which do not reach so deep into the parameter stack.
2DROP	Discard the top two items on the parameter stack.
2DUP	Duplicate the top two items on the parameter stack.
+	Add the top item on the parameter to the second item, and then pops the top item off the parameter stack. It is recoded in assembly for speed.
INVERT	Invert each individual bit in the top item on the parameter stack. It is often called 1's complement operation.

ROT is unique in that it accesses the third item on the data stack. All other stack operators can only access one or two stack items. In Forth programming, it is generally accepted that one should not try to access stack items deeper than the third item. When you have to access deeper into the data stack, it is a good time to re-evaluate your algorithm. Most often, you can avoid this situation by factoring your code into smaller parts which do not reach so deep.

```
;   NEGATE ( n -- -n )
; Two's complement of tos.

 COLON 6,"NEGATE"
NEGAT:
 RCALL INVER  adiw tosl,1  ret

;   DNEGATE ( d -- -d )
; Two's complement of top double.

 COLON 7,"DNEGATE" DNEGA:
 RCALL INVER  RCALL TOR
 RCALL INVER
 RCALL DOLIT  .DW 1
 RCALL UPLUS
```

```
 RCALL RFROM
 RJMP PLUS

;  - ( n1 n2 -- n1-n2 ) ; Subtraction.

 COLON 1,"-"
SUBB:
   ld  temp0, Y+    ld  temp1, Y+
   sub  temp0, tosl    sbc  temp1, tosh
   movw  tosl, temp0
   ret

;  ABS  ( n -- n )
; Return the absolute value of n.

 COLON 3,"ABS"
ABSS:
 RCALL DUPP
 RCALL ZLESS
 RCALL QBRAN  .DW ABS1  RJMP NEGAT ABS1:
 RET
```

NEGATE	Negate the top item on the parameter stack. It is often called 2's complement operation.
DNEGATE	Negate the top two items on the parameter stack, as a 32-bit double integer.
-	Subtract the top item on the parameter stack from the second item, and then pops the top item off the parameter stack.
ABS	Replace the top item on the parameter stack with its absolute value.

5.2.2 Comparison

The primitive comparison commands in 328eForth are ?branch and 0<. However, ?branch is at such a low level that it is not used in compound commands. ?branch is secretly compiled into compound commands by IF as an address literal. For all intentions and purposes, we can consider IF the equivalent of ?branch. When IF is encountered, the top item on the parameter stack is considered a logic flag. If it is true (non-zero), the execution continues until ELSE, then jump to THEN, or to THEN directly if there is no ELSE clause.

The following logic words are constructed using the IF...ELSE...THEN structure with 0< and XOR. XOR is used as a "not equal" operator, because if the top two items on the parameter stack are not equal, the XOR operator will return a non-zero number, which is considered to be true.

```
;  = ( w w -- t )
; Return true if top two are equal.

 COLON 1,"="
EQUAL:
 RCALL XORR
 RCALL QBRAN
 .DW  EQU1
 RCALL DOLIT
 .DW  0
 RET
EQU1:
 RCALL DOLIT
 .DW  -1
 RET

;  U< ( u u -- t )
; Unsigned compare of top two items.

 COLON 2,"U<"
ULESS:
 RCALL DDUP
 RCALL XORR
 RCALL ZLESS
 RCALL QBRAN
 .DW  ULES1
 RCALL SWAPP
 RCALL DROP
 RJMP ZLESS
ULES1:
 RCALL SUBB
```

```
 RJMP ZLESS

;  < ( n1 n2 -- t )
; Signed compare of top two items.

 COLON 1,"<"
LESS:
 RCALL DDUP
 RCALL XORR
 RCALL ZLESS
 RCALL QBRAN
 .DW  LESS1
 RCALL DROP
 RJMP ZLESS
LESS1:
 RCALL SUBB
 RJMP ZLESS
```

=	Compare top two items on the parameter stack. If they are equal, replace these two items with a true flag; otherwise, replace them with a false flag.
U<	Compare two unsigned numbers on the top of the parameter stack. If the top item is less than the second item in unsigned comparison, replace these two items with a true flag; otherwise, replace them with a false flag. This command is very important, especially in comparing addresses, as we
	assume that the addresses are unsigned numbers pointing to unique memory locations. The arithmetic comparison operator < cannot be used to determine whether one address is higher or lower than the other. Using < for address comparison had been the single cause of many failures in the annals of FORTH. We don not have this problem in ATmega328P since it has only 32 KB of flash memory. However, watch out when you move 328eForth to a bigger chip.
<	Compare two signed numbers on the top of the parameter stack. If the top item is less than the second item in signed comparison, replace these two items with a true flag; otherwise, replace them with a false flag.

```
;   MAX ( n n -- n )
; Return the greater of two top stack items.

 COLON 3,"MAX"
MAX:
 RCALL DDUP
 RCALL LESS
 RCALL QBRAN  .DW  MAX1  RCALL SWAPP
MAX1:
 RJMP DROP

;   MIN ( n n -- n )
; Return the smaller of top two stack items.

 COLON 3,"MIN"
MIN:
 RCALL DDUP
 RCALL SWAPP
 RCALL LESS
 RCALL QBRAN
 .DW  MIN1
 RCALL SWAPP
MIN1:
 RJMP DROP

;   WITHIN ( u ul uh -- t )
; Return true if u is within the range
; of ul and uh. ( ul <= u < uh )
 COLON 6,"WITHIN"
WITHI:
 RCALL OVER
 RCALL SUBB
 RCALL TOR
 RCALL SUBB
 RCALL RFROM
 RJMP ULESS
```

MAX	Retain the larger of the top two items on the parameter stack. Both numbers are assumed to be signed integers.
MIN	Retain the smaller of the top two items on the parameter stack. Both numbers are assumed to be signed integers.
WITHIN	Check whether the third item on the parameter stack is within the range as specified by the top two numbers on the parameter stack. The range is inclusive as to the lower limit and exclusive to the upper limit. If the third item is within range, a true flag is returned on the parameter stack, replacing all three items. Otherwise, a false flag is returned. All numbers are assumed to be signed integers.

5.2.3 Divide

UM/MOD and UM* are the most complicated and comprehensive division and multiplication commands. Once they are coded, all other division and multiplication operators can be derived easily from them. It has been a tradition in FORTH programming that one solves the most difficult problem first, and all other problems are solved by themselves.

```
;; Divide

;  UM/MOD ( udl udh un -- ur uq )
; Unsigned divide of a double by a single.
; Return mod and quotient.

 COLON 6,"UM/MOD"
UMMOD:
   movw  temp4, tosl
   ld    temp2, Y+
   ld    temp3, Y+
   ld    temp0, Y+
   ld    temp1, Y+

;; unsigned 32/16 -> 16r16 divide
  ; set  loop counter
   ldi  temp6,$10 UMMOD1:
   ; shift left, saving high bit
   clr  temp7
```

```
    lsl  temp0
    rol  temp1
    rol  temp2
    rol  temp3
    rol  temp7
  ; try subtracting divisor
    cp   temp2, temp4
    cpc  temp3, temp5
    cpc  temp7,zerol
    brcs  UMMOD3 UMMOD2:
    ; dividend is large enough
    ; do the subtraction for real
    ; and set lowest bit
    inc  temp0
    sub  temp2, temp4
    sbc  temp3, temp5
UMMOD3:
    dec   temp6
    brne  UMMOD1
UMMOD4:
```

```
    ; put remainder on stack
    st   -Y,temp3
    st   -Y,temp2
    ; put quotient on stack
    movw  tosl, temp0
    ret

;   M/MOD ( d n -- r q )
; Signed floored divide of double by single.
; Return mod and quotient.

 COLON 5,"M/MOD"
MSMOD:
 RCALL DUPP
 RCALL ZLESS
 RCALL DUPP
 RCALL TOR
 RCALL QBRAN
 .DW MMOD1
 RCALL NEGAT
 RCALL TOR
 RCALL DNEGA
 RCALL RFROM
MMOD1:
 RCALL TOR
```

```
 RCALL DUPP
 RCALL ZLESS
 RCALL QBRAN
 .DW MMOD2
 RCALL RAT
 RCALL PLUS
MMOD2:
 RCALL RFROM
 RCALL UMMOD
 RCALL RFROM
 RCALL QBRAN
 .DW MMOD3
 RCALL SWAPP
 RCALL NEGAT
 RCALL SWAPP
MMOD3:
 RET

;   /MOD ( n n -- r q )
; Signed divide. Return mod and quotient.

 COLON 4,"/MOD"
SLMOD:
 RCALL OVER
 RCALL ZLESS
 RCALL SWAPP
 RJMP MSMOD

;   MOD ( n n -- r )
; Signed divide. Return mod only.

 COLON 3,"MOD"
MODD:
 RCALL SLMOD
 RJMP DROP

;   / ( n n -- q )
; Signed divide. Return quotient only.
 COLON 1,"/"
 RCALL SLMOD
 RCALL SWAPP
RJMP DROP
```

UM/MOD	Divide an unsigned double integer by an unsigned single integer. It returns the unsigned remainder and unsigned quotient on the parameter stack. It is coded in assembly and the double integer dividend is stored in 4 registers temp0 to temp3. Division is carried out similar to long hand division.
M/MOD	Divide a signed double integer by a signed single integer. It returns the signed remainder and signed quotient on the parameter stack. The signed division is floored towards negative infinity.
/MOD	Divide a signed single integer by a signed integer. It replaces these two items with the signed remainder and quotient.
MOD	Divide a signed single integer by a signed integer. It replaces these two items with the signed remainder only.
/	Divide a signed single integer by a signed integer. It replaces these two items with the signed quotient only.

5.2.4 Multiply

```
;; Multiply

;  UM* ( u u -- ud )
; Unsigned multiply. Return double product.

 COLON 3,"UM*"
UMSTA:
  movw  temp0, tosl
  loadtos     ; low bytes
  mul  tosl,temp0
  movw  zl, r0
  clr  temp2
  clr  temp3    ; middle bytes
  mul  tosh, temp0
  add  zh, r0
  adc  temp2, r1
  adc  temp3, zeroh
  mul  tosl, temp1
```

```
add zh, r0
adc temp2, r1
adc temp3, zeroh
mul tosh, temp1
add temp2, r0
```

```
adc temp3, r1
movw tosl, zl
savetos movw tosl,
temp2 ret

; * ( n n -- n )
; Signed multiply. Return single product.

COLON 1,"*"
STAR:
RCALL MSTAR
RJMP DROP

; M* ( n n -- d )
; Signed multiply. Return double product.

COLON 2,"M*"
MSTAR:
RCALL DDUP
RCALL XORR
RCALL ZLESS
RCALL TOR
RCALL ABSS
RCALL SWAPP
RCALL ABSS
RCALL UMSTA
RCALL RFROM
RCALL QBRAN
.DW MSTA1
RCALL DNEGA
MSTA1:
RET

; */MOD ( n1 n2 n3 -- r q )
; Multiply n1 and n2, then divide by n3.
; Return mod and quotient.

COLON 5,"*/MOD"
SSMOD:
```

```
      RCALL TOR
      RCALL MSTAR

RCAL
L
RFRO
M
      RJMP MSMOD

     ;  */ ( n1 n2 n3 -- q )
     ; Multiply n1 by n2, then divide by n3.
     ; Return quotient only.

      COLON 2,"*/"
     STASL:
      RCALL SSMOD
      RCALL SWAPP
      RJMP DROP
```

UM*	Multiply two unsigned single integers and returns the unsigned double integer product on the parameter stack. UM* command takes advantage of
	the multiply machine instructions in ATmega328P chip. The multiply instructions in ATmega328P operate on 8 bit values, and the 16 bit products have to be added properly to form a 32 bit double integer product.
*	Multiply two signed single integers and returns the signed single integer product on the parameter stack.
M*	Multiply two signed single integers and returns the signed double integer product on the parameter stack.
*/MOD	Multiply the signed integers n1 and n2, and then divides the double integer product by n3. It in fact is ratioing n1 by n2/n3. It returns both the remainder and the quotient.
*/	Multiply the signed integers n1 and n2, and then divides the double integer product by n3. It returns only the quotient.

FORTH is very close to assembly languages in that it generally only handles integer numbers. There are floating point extensions in many more sophisticated FORTH systems, but they are more exceptions than rules. The reason why FORTH has traditionally been an integer language is that integers are handled faster and more efficiently in the computers, and most technical problems can be solved satisfactorily only using integers. A 16-bit integer has the dynamic range of 110 dB which is far more than enough for most engineering problems. The precision of a 16-bit integer representation is limited to one part in 65535, which could be inadequate for small numbers. However, the precision can be greatly improved by scaling; i.e., taking the ratio of two integers. It was demonstrated that pi, or any other irrational numbers, can be represented accurately to 1 part in 100,000,000 by a ratio of two 16-bit integers.

The scaling commands */MOD and */ are useful in scaling number n1 by the ratio of n2/n3. When n2 and n3 are properly chosen, the scaling commands can preserve precision similar to the floating point operations at a much higher speed. Notice also that in these scaling operations, the intermediate product of n1 and n2 is a double precision integer so that the precision of scaling is maintained.

5.2.5 Miscellaneous

```
;; Miscellaneous

;   >CHAR ( c -- c )
; Filter non-printing characters.

; COLON 5,">CHAR" TCHAR:
 RCALL DUPP
 RCALL BLANK
 RCALL DOLIT  .DW  $7F
 RCALL WITHI
 RCALL QBRAN
 .DW  TCHAR1
 RET
TCHAR1:
 RCALL DROP
```

```
 RCALL DOLIT
 .DW '_'
 RET

;  DEPTH ( -- n )
; Return the depth of the data stack.

 COLON 5,"DEPTH"
DEPTH:
 RCALL SPAT
 RCALL DOLIT
 .DW  SPP-2
 RCALL SWAPP
 RCALL SUBB
 RJMP TWOSL

;  PICK ( ... +n -- ... w )
; Copy the nth stack item to tos.

 COLON 4,"PICK"
PICK:
 ADIW TOSL,1  RCALL CELLS
 RCALL SPAT
 RCALL PLUS
 RJMP AT
```

>CHAR	Convert a non-printable character to a harmless underscore character(ASCII 95). As 328eForth is designed to communicate with a host computer through a serial I/O device, it is important that 328eForth will not emit control characters to the host and thereby causes unexpected behavior on the host computer. >CHAR thus filters the characters before they are sent out by EMIT.
DEPTH	Push the number of items currently on the parameter stack to the top of the stack.

PICK	Take a number n off the parameter stack and replaces it with the n'th item on the parameter stack. The number n is 0-based; i.e., the top item is number 0, the next item is number 1, etc. Therefore, 0 PICK is equivalent to DUP, and 1 PICK is equivalent to OVER.

5.2.6 Memory Access

A memory array is generally specified by its starting address and its length in bytes. In a count string, the first byte is a count byte, specifying the number of bytes in the following string. String literals in compound commands and the name strings in the headers of command records are all represented by count strings. Following commands are useful in accessing memory arrays and strings.

```
;; Memory access

;  +! ( n a -- )
; Add n to the contents at address a.

 COLON 2,"+!"
PSTOR:
 RCALL SWAPP
 RCALL OVER
 RCALL AT
 RCALL PLUS
 RCALL SWAPP
 RJMP STORE

;  COUNT ( b -- b +n )
; Return count byte of a string and add 1 to
; byte address.

 COLON 5,"COUNT"
COUNT:
 movw zl, tosl
 ld  temp0, z+
 movw tosl, zl
 savetos
 mov  tosl, temp0
 clr  tosh
```

```
 ret

;  ICOUNT ( b -- b +n )
; Return count byte of a string and add 1
; to byte address.

 COLON 6,"ICOUNT"
ICOUNT:
 RCALL DUPP
 adiw tosl,1
 RCALL SWAPP
 RJMP ICAT

;  HERE ( -- a )
; Return the top of the code dictionary.

 COLON 4,"HERE"
HEREE:
 RCALL DPP
 RJMP AT

;  PAD ( -- a )
; Return the address of the text buffer
; above the code dictionary.

 COLON 3,"PAD"
PAD:
 RCALL HEREE
 RCALL DOLIT
 .DW  $40
 RJMP PLUS
```

+!	Add the second item on the parameter stack to the cell addressed by the top item on the stack.
COUNT	Fetch one byte from RAM memory pointed to by the address on the top of the parameter stack. This address is incremented by 1, and the byte just read is pushed on the stack. COUNT is designed to get the count byte at

	the beginning of a counted string, and returns the address of the first byte in the string and the length of this string. However, it is often used in a loop to read consecutive bytes in a byte array.
ICOUNT	Fetch one byte from flash memory pointed to by the address on the top of the parameter stack. This address is incremented by 1, and the byte just read is pushed on the stack. ICOUNT is used to access counted strings stored in flash memory.
HERE	Push the address of the first free location in the RAM memory. FORTH text interpreter stores here a string parsed out of the Terminal Input Buffer and then searches the dictionary for a command with this name.
PAD	Push on the parameter stack the address of the text buffer where numbers to be output are constructed and text strings are stored temporarily. It is 64 bytes above HERE.

```
;  TIB ( -- a )
; Return the address of the terminal
; input buffer.

 COLON 3,"TIB"
TIB:
 RCALL NTIB
 ADIW TOSL,2
 RJMP AT

;  @EXECUTE ( a -- )
; Execute vector stored in address a.

 COLON 8,"@EXECUTE" ATEXE:
 RCALL AT
 RCALL QDUP ;?address or zero
 RCALL QBRAN
 .DW  EXE1
 RCALL EXECU ;execute if non-zero
EXE1:
 RET   ;do nothing if zero
```

```
;   CMOVE ( b1 b2 u -- )
; Copy u bytes from b1 to b2.

 COLON 5,"CMOVE"
CMOVE:
 RCALL TOR
 RJMP CMOV2
CMOV1:
 RCALL TOR
 RCALL COUNT
 RCALL RAT
 RCALL CSTOR
 RCALL RFROM
 ADIW TOSL,1
CMOV2:
 RCALL DONXT
 .DW  CMOV1
 RJMP DDROP

; UPPER ( c -- c' )
; Change character to upper case

; COLON 5,"UPPER" UPPER:
 RCALL DUPP
 RCALL DOLIT
 .DW  $61
 RCALL DOLIT
 .DW  $7B
 RCALL WITHI
 RCALL QBRAN
 .DW  UPPER1
 RCALL DOLIT
 .DW  $5F
 RCALL ANDD
UPPER1:
 RET
```

```
;  FILL ( b u c -- )
; Fill u bytes of character c to area
; beginning at b.

 COLON 4,"FILL"
FILL:
 RCALL SWAPP
 RCALL TOR
 RCALL SWAPP
 RJMP FILL2
FILL1:
 RCALL DDUP
 RCALL CSTOR
 ADIW TOSL,1
FILL2:
 RCALL DONXT
 .DW  FILL1
 RJMP DDROP
```

TIB	Push the address of the Terminal Input Buffer on the parameter stack. Terminal Input Buffer stores a line of text from the serial I/O input device. FORTH text interpreter then processes or interprets this line of text.
@EXECUTE	Fetch a code field address of a command which is stored in the address on the top of the parameter stack, and jumps to it to execute this command. It is used extensively to execute vectored commands stored in RAM memory. The behavior of a vectored command can be changed dynamically at the run time.
CMOVE	Copy a byte array from one location to another in RAM memory. The top three item on the parameter stack are the source address, the destination address and the number of bytes to be copied.

UPPER	Convert the ASCII character on the top of the parameter stack to an upper case character. This command is used to convert input text string to an upper case string so that the text interpreter is now case insensitive.
FILL	Fill a memory array with the same byte. The top three items on the parameter stack are the address of the array, the length of the array in bytes, and the byte value to be filled into this array.

5.3 Input Output

5.3.1 Numeric Output

FORTH is interesting in its special capabilities in handling numbers across a man-machine interface. It recognizes that machines and humans prefer very different representations of numbers. Machines prefer binary representation, but humans prefer decimal Arabic representation. However, depending on circumstances, a human may want numbers to be represented in other radices, like hexadecimal, octal, and sometimes binary.

FORTH solves this problem of internal (machine) versus external (human) number representations by insisting that all numbers are represented in binary form in CPU and memory. Only when numbers are imported or exported for human consumption are they converted to external ASCII representation. The radix of the external representation is stored in system variable BASE. You can select any reasonable radix in BASE, up to 72, limited by available printable characters in the ASCII character set.

The output number string is built below the PAD buffer in RAM memory. The least significant digit is extracted from the integer on the top of the parameter stack by dividing it by the current radix in BASE. The digit thus extracted is added to the output string backwards from PAD to the low memory. The conversion is terminated when the integer is divided to zero. The address and length of the number string are made available by #> for outputting.

An output number conversion is initiated by <# and terminated by #>. Between them, # converts one digit at a time, #S converts all the digits, while HOLD and SIGN inserts special characters into the string under construction. This set of commands is very versatile and can handle many different output formats.

```
;; Numeric output, single precision

;  DIGIT ( u -- c )
; Convert digit u to a character.

; COLON 5,"DIGIT" DIGIT:
 RCALL DOLIT
 .DW  9
 RCALL OVER
 RCALL LESS
 RCALL DOLIT
 .DW  7
 RCALL ANDD
 RCALL PLUS
 RCALL DOLIT
 .DW  '0'
 RJMP PLUS

;  EXTRACT ( n base -- n c )
; Extract the least significant digit from n.

; COLON 7,"EXTRACT" EXTRC:
 RCALL DOLIT  .DW  0
 RCALL SWAPP
 RCALL UMMOD
 RCALL SWAPP  RJMP DIGIT

;  <# ( -- )
; Initiate the numeric output process.

 COLON 2,"<#"
BDIGS:
 RCALL PAD
 RCALL HLD
 RJMP STORE

;  HOLD ( c -- )
; Insert a character into the numeric output string.
```

```
 COLON 4,"HOLD"
HOLD:
 RCALL HLD
 RCALL AT
 SBIW TOSL,1
 RCALL DUPP
 RCALL HLD
 RCALL STORE  RJMP
CSTOR
```

DIGIT	Convert an integer digit to the corresponding ASCII character.
EXTRACT	Extract the least significant digit from a number n on the top of the parameter stack. n is divided by the radix in BASE and the extracted digit is converted to its ASCII character which is pushed on the parameter stack.
<#	Initiate the output number onversion process by storing PAD buffer address into system variable HLD, which points to the location next numeric digit will be stored.
HOLD	Append an ASCII character whose code is on the top of the parameter stack, to the numeric out put string at HLD. HLD is decremented to receive the next digit.

```
;  # ( u -- u )
; Extract one digit from u and append the
; digit to output string.

 COLON 1,"#"

DIG:
 RCALL BASE
 RCALL AT
 RCALL EXTRC
 RJMP HOLD

;  #S ( u -- 0 )
```

```
; Convert u until all digits are added
; to the output string.

 COLON 2,"#S"
DIGS:
DIGS1:
 RCALL DIG
 RCALL DUPP
 RCALL QBRAN
 .DW  DIGS2
 RJMP DIGS1
DIGS2:
 RET

;   SIGN ( n -- )
; Add a minus sign to the numeric
; output string.

 COLON 4,"SIGN"
SIGN:
 RCALL ZLESS
 RCALL QBRAN
 .DW  SIGN1
 RCALL DOLIT
 .DW  '-'
 RCALL HOLD
SIGN1: RET

;   #> ( w -- b u )
; Prepare the output string to be TYPE'd.

 COLON 2,"#>"
EDIGS:
 RCALL DROP
 RCALL HLD
 RCALL AT
 RCALL PAD
 RCALL OVER
 RJMP SUBB
```

#	Extract one digit from integer on the top of the parameter stack, according to radix in BASE, and add it to output numeric string.
#S	Extract all digits to output string until the integer on the top of the parameter stack is 0.
SIGN	Insert a - sign into the numeric output string if the integer on the top of the parameter stack is negative.
#>	Terminate the numeric conversion and pushes the address and length of output numeric string on the parameter stack.

```
;  str ( w -- b u )
; Convert a signed integer to
; a numeric string.

; COLON 3,"str" STR:
 RCALL DUPP
 RCALL TOR
 RCALL ABSS
 RCALL BDIGS
 RCALL DIGS
 RCALL RFROM
 RCALL SIGN
 RJMP EDIGS

;  HEX ( -- )
; Use radix 16 as base for
; numeric conversions.

 COLON 3,"HEX"
HEX:
 RCALL DOLIT
 .DW 16
 RCALL BASE
 RJMP STORE

;  DECIMAL ( -- )
; Use radix 10 as base for
; numeric conversions.

 COLON 7,"DECIMAL"
```

```
DECIM:
 RCALL DOLIT
 .DW 10
 RCALL BASE
 RJMP STORE
```

str	Convert a signed integer on the top of the parameter stack to a numeric output string.
HEX	Set numeric conversion radix to 16 for hexadecimal conversions.
DECIMAL	Set numeric conversion radix to 10 for decimal conversions.

5.3.2 Numeric Input

The 328eForth text interpreter must handle numbers input to the system. It parses commands out of the input stream and executes them in sequence. When the text interpreter encounters a string which is not the name of a command in the dictionary, it assumes that the string must be a number and attempts to convert the ASCII digit string to a number according to the current radix. When the text interpreter succeeds in converting the string to a number, the number is pushed on the parameter stack for future use, if the text interpreter is in the interpreting mode. If it is in the compiling mode, the text interpreter will compile the number to the dictionary as an integer literal so that when the command under construction is later executed, the integer value will be pushed on the parameter stack.

If the text interpreter fails to convert the string to a number, this is an error condition which will cause the text interpreter to abort, post an error message to you, and then wait for your next line of commands.

```
;; Numeric input, single precision

;   DIGIT? ( c base -- u t )
; Convert a character to its numeric value.
; A flag indicates success.
```

```
; COLON 6,"DIGIT?" DIGTQ:
 RCALL TOR
 RCALL DOLIT
 .DW '0'
 RCALL SUBB
 RCALL DOLIT
 .DW 9
 RCALL OVER
 RCALL LESS
 RCALL QBRAN
 .DW DGTQ1 RCALL DOLIT
 .DW 7
 RCALL SUBB
 RCALL DUPP
 RCALL DOLIT
 .DW 10
 RCALL LESS
 RCALL ORR
DGTQ1:
 RCALL DUPP
 RCALL RFROM  RJMP ULESS

;   NUMBER? ( a -- n T | a F )
; Convert a number string to integer.
; Push a flag on tos.

 COLON 7,"NUMBER?"
NUMBQ:
 RCALL BASE
 RCALL AT
 RCALL TOR
 RCALL DOLIT
 .DW 0
 RCALL OVER
 RCALL COUNT
 RCALL OVER
 RCALL CAT
 RCALL DOLIT
 .DW '$'
 RCALL EQUAL
 RCALL QBRAN
 .DW NUMQ1
 RCALL HEX
```

```
 RCALL SWAPP
 adiw tosl,1
 RCALL SWAPP
 sbiw tosl,1
NUMQ1:
```

```
RCALL OVER
 RCALL CAT
 RCALL DOLIT

 .DW '-'
 RCALL EQUAL
 RCALL TOR
 RCALL SWAPP
 RCALL RAT
 RCALL SUBB
 RCALL SWAPP
 RCALL RAT
 RCALL PLUS
 RCALL QDUP
 RCALL QBRAN
 .DW NUMQ6
 sbiw tosl,1
 RCALL TOR
NUMQ2:
 RCALL DUPP
 RCALL TOR
 RCALL CAT
 RCALL BASE
 RCALL AT
 RCALL DIGTQ
 RCALL QBRAN
 .DW NUMQ4
 RCALL SWAPP
 RCALL BASE
 RCALL AT
 RCALL STAR
 RCALL PLUS
 RCALL RFROM
 adiw tosl,1
 RCALL DONXT
 .DW NUMQ2
 RCALL DROP
 RCALL RAT
 RCALL QBRAN
```

```
 .DW  NUMQ3
 RCALL NEGAT
NUMQ3:
 RCALL SWAPP
 RJMP NUMQ5
NUMQ4:
 RCALL RFROM
 RCALL RFROM
 RCALL DDROP
 RCALL DDROP
 RCALL DOLIT
 .DW  0
NUMQ5:
 RCALL DUPP
NUMQ6:
 RCALL RFROM
 RCALL DDROP
 RCALL RFROM
 RCALL BASE
  RJMP STORE
```

DIGIT?	Convert an ASCII numeric digit c on the top of the parameter stack to its numeric value u according to current radix b. If conversion is successful, push a true flag above u. If not successful, return c and a false flag.

NUMBER?	Convert a count string of ASCII numeric digits at location a to an integer. If first character is a $, convert in hexadecimal; otherwise, convert using radix in BASE. If first character is a -, negate converted integer. If an illegal character is encountered, the address of string and a false flag are pushed on the parameter stack. Successful conversion pushes integer value and a true flag on the parameter stack. NUMBER? is very complicated because it has to cover many formats in the input numeric string. It also has to detect the error condition when it encounters an illegal numeric digit. .

5.3.3 Basic I/O

328eForth system assumes that it communicates with its environment only through a serial I/O interface. To support the serial I/O, only three words are needed:

```
;; Basic I/O

;  KEY ( -- c )
; Wait for and return an input character.

 COLON 3,"KEY"
KEY:
KEY1:
 RCALL QRX
 RCALL QBRAN
 .DW  KEY1
 RET

;  SPACE ( -- )
; Send the blank character to the
; output device.

 COLON 5,"SPACE"
SPACE:
```

```
 RCALL BLANK
 RJMP EMIT

;   CHARS ( +n c -- )
; Send n characters to the output device.

; COLON 5,"CHARS"
CHARS:
 RCALL SWAPP
 RCALL TOR
 RJMP CHAR2
CHAR1:
 RCALL DUPP
 RCALL EMIT
CHAR2:
 RCALL DONXT
 .DW  CHAR1
 RJMP DROP

;   SPACES ( +n -- )
; Send n spaces to the output device.

 COLON 6,"SPACES"
SPACS:
 RCALL BLANK
 RJMP CHARS
```

?KEY	Return a false flag if no character is pending in the receiver. If a character is received, the character and a true flag are returned.
KEY	Execute ?KEY continually until a valid character is received and the character is returned.
EMIT	Send a character out through the transmit line.
SPACE	Output a blank (space) character, ASCII 32.
CHARS	Output n ASCII characters. The ASCII code is on the top of the parameter stack, and number n is the second item on the parameter stack

SPACES	Output n blank (space) characters.

```
;   TYPE ( b u -- )
; Output u characters from b.

 COLON 4,"TYPE"
TYPES:
 RCALL TOR
 RJMP TYPE2
TYPE1:
 RCALL COUNT
 RCALL TCHAR
 RCALL EMIT
TYPE2:
 RCALL DONXT
 .DW  TYPE1
 RJMP DROP

;   ITYPE ( b u -- )
; Output u characters from b.

 COLON 5,"ITYPE"
ITYPES:
 RCALL TOR
 RJMP ITYPE2
ITYPE1:
 RCALL ICOUNT
 RCALL TCHAR
 RCALL EMIT
ITYPE2:
 RCALL DONXT
 .DW  ITYPE1
 RJMP DROP

;   CR ( -- )
; Output a carriage return and a line feed.
 COLON 2,"CR"
CR:
 RCALL DOLIT
 .DW  CRR
 RCALL EMIT
 RCALL DOLIT
 .DW  LF
```

```
        RJMP EMIT
```

TYPE	Output n characters from a string in RAM memory. The second item on the parameter stack is the address of the string array, and the length in bytes is on the top of the parameter stack.
ITYPE	Output n characters from a string in the flash memory. The second item on the parameter stack is the address of the string array, and the length in bytes is on the top of the parameter stack.
CR	Output a carriage-return and a line-feed, ASCII 13 and 10.

String literals are data structures compiled in compound command, in-line with other tokens, literal structures, and control structures. A string literal must start with a string token which knows how to handle the following string at run time. Here are two examples of string literals:

```
: xxx    ...   $" A compiled string"  ...   ;
: yyy    ...   ." An output string"  ...   ;
```

In compound command xxx, $" is an immediate command which compiles the following string as a string literal preceded by a special token $"|. When $"| is executed at run time, it returns the address of this string on the parameter stack. In yyy, ." compiles a string literal preceded by another token ."|, which prints the compiled string to the output device at run time.

```
; do$ ( -- a )
; Return the address of a compiled string.

; COLON COMPO+3,"do$" DOSTR:
 RCALL RFROM ;ra
 RCALL RFROM ;ra a
 RCALL DUPP ;ra a a
 RCALL DUPP ;ra a a a
 movw zl,tosl
 readflashcell tosl,tosh
 clr  tosh ;ra a a count
```

```
RCALL TWOSL
RCALL PLUS
ADIW TOSL,1 ;ra a a'
```

```
 RCALL TOR ;ra a
 RCALL SWAPP ;a ra
 RCALL TOR ;a
 RCALL CELLS ;byte address
 RET

;  $"| ( -- a )
; Run time routine compiled by $".
; Return address of a compiled string.

; COLON COMPO+3,'$'
; .DB  '"','|'
STRQP:
 RCALL DOSTR
 RET    ;force a call to do$

;  ."| ( -- )
; Run time routine of ." .
; Output a compiled string.

; COLON COMPO+3,'.'
; .DB  '"','|'
DOTQP:
 RCALL DOSTR
 RCALL ICOUNT
 RJMP ITYPES

;  .R  ( n +n -- )
; Display an integer in a field of n columns,
; right justified.

 COLON 2,".R"
DOTR:
 RCALL TOR
 RCALL STR
 RCALL RFROM
 RCALL OVER
 RCALL SUBB
 RCALL SPACS
 RJMP TYPES
```

do$	Push the address of a string literal on the parameter stack. It is called by a string token like $"| or ."|, which precede their respective strings in flash memory. Therefore, the second item on the return stack points to the string. This address is pushed on the parameter stack. This second item on the return stack must be modified so that it will point to the next token after the string literal. This way. the token after the string literal will be executed, skipping over the string literal. Both $"\| and ."\| use the word do$, which retrieve the address of a string stored as the second item on the return stack.
$"|	Push the address of the following string on the parameter stack, and then executes the token immediately following the string.
."|	Print the following string, and then executes the token immediately following the string.
.R	Print a signed integer n , the second item on the parameter stack, right-justified in a field of +n characters. +n is on the top of the parameter stack.

```
; U.R ( u +n -- )
; Display an unsigned integer in n column,
; right justified.

 COLON 3,"U.R"
UDOTR:
 RCALL TOR
 RCALL BDIGS
 RCALL DIGS
 RCALL EDIGS
 RCALL RFROM
 RCALL OVER
 RCALL SUBB
 RCALL SPACS
 RJMP TYPES

; U. ( u -- )
; Display an unsigned integer in free format.

 COLON 2,"U."
```

```
UDOT:
 RCALL BDIGS
 RCALL DIGS
 RCALL EDIGS
 RCALL SPACE
 RJMP TYPES

; . ( w -- )
; Display an integer in free format,
; preceeded by a space.

 COLON 1,"."
DOT:
 RCALL BASE
 RCALL AT
 RCALL DOLIT
 .DW 10
 RCALL XORR ;?decimal
 RCALL QBRAN
 .DW DOT1
 RJMP UDOT
DOT1:
 RCALL STR
 RCALL SPACE
 RJMP TYPES

; ? ( a -- )
; Display the contents in a memory cell.

 COLON 1,"?"
QUEST:
 RCALL AT
 RJMP DOT
```

With the number formatting command set as shown above, one can format numbers for output in any format desired. The free output format is a number string preceded by a single space. The fix column format displays a number right-justified in a column of a pre-determined width. The commands ' . ' , 'U.', and ? use the free format. The words .R and U.R use the fix format.

U.R	Print an unsigned integer n right-justified in a field of +n characters.
U.	Print an unsigned integer u in free format, followed by a space.
.	Print a signed integer n in free format, followed by a space.
?	Print signed integer stored in memory a on the top of the parameter stack, in free format followed by a space.

5.3.4 Parsing

Parsing is always considered a very advanced topic in computer science. However, because FORTH uses very simple syntax rules, parsing is easy. FORTH input stream consists of ASCII strings separated by spaces and other white space characters like tabs, carriage returns, and line feeds. The text interpreter scans the input stream, parses out strings, and interprets them in sequence. After a string is parsed out of the input stream, the text interpreter will 'interpret' it; i.e., execute it if it is a valid command, compile it if the text interpreter is in the compiling mode, and convert it to a number if the string is not a FORTH command.

parse is the elementary command to do text parsing. From the input stream, which starts at b1 and is of u1 characters long, it parses out the first text string delimited by character c. It returns the address b2 and length u2 of the string just parsed out and the difference n between b1 and b2. Leading delimiters are skipped over.

The case where the delimiting character is a space (ASCII 32) is special, because this is when the text interpreter is parsing for valid commands. It thus must skip over leading space characters. When parse is used to compile string literals, it will use the double quot character (ASCII 34) as the delimiting character. It the delimiting character is not space, parse starts scanning immediately, looking for the designated delimiting character.

```
;; Parsing

;   parse ( b u c -- b u delta ; <string> )
; Scan string delimited by c. Return found
; string and its offset.

; COLON 5,"parse" PARS:
 RCALL TEMP
 RCALL STORE
 RCALL OVER  RCALL TOR
 RCALL DUPP
 RCALL QBRAN
 .DW  PARS8
 SBIW TOSL,1
 RCALL TEMP
```

```
 RCALL CAT
 RCALL BLANK
 RCALL EQUAL
 RCALL QBRAN
 .DW  PARS3
 RCALL TOR
PARS1:
 RCALL BLANK
 RCALL OVER
 RCALL CAT ;skip leading blanks ONLY
 RCALL SUBB
 RCALL ZLESS
 RCALL INVER
 RCALL QBRAN
 .DW  PARS2
 ADIW TOSL,1
 RCALL DONXT
 .DW  PARS1
 RCALL RFROM
 RCALL DROP
 RCALL DOLIT
 .DW  0
 RCALL DUPP
 RET
PARS2:
 RCALL RFROM
PARS3:
 RCALL OVER
```

```
 RCALL SWAPP
 RCALL TOR
PARS4:
 RCALL TEMP
 RCALL CAT
 RCALL OVER
 RCALL CAT
 RCALL SUBB ;scan for delimiter
 RCALL TEMP
 RCALL CAT
 RCALL BLANK
 RCALL EQUAL
 RCALL QBRAN
 .DW  PARS5
 RCALL ZLESS
PARS5:
 RCALL QBRAN
 .DW  PARS6
 ADIW TOSL,1
 RCALL DONXT
 .DW  PARS4
 RCALL DUPP
 RCALL TOR
 RJMP PARS7
PARS6:
 RCALL RFROM
 RCALL DROP
 RCALL DUPP
 ADIW TOSL,1
 RCALL TOR
```

```
PARS7:
 RCALL OVER
 RCALL SUBB
 RCALL RFROM
 RCALL RFROM
 RJMP SUBB
PARS8:
 RCALL OVER
 RCALL RFROM
 RJMP SUBB

;   PARSE ( c -- b u ; <string> )
; Scan input stream and return counted
; string delimited by c.
```

```
; COLON 5,"PARSE"
PARSE:
 RCALL TOR
 RCALL TIB
 RCALL INN
 RCALL AT
 RCALL PLUS ;current input buffer pointer
 RCALL NTIB
 RCALL AT
 RCALL INN
 RCALL AT
 RCALL SUBB ;remaining count
 RCALL RFROM
 RCALL PARS
 RCALL INN
 RJMP PSTOR

;  .( ( -- )
; Output following string up to next ) .

 COLON IMEDD+2,".("
DOTPR:
 RCALL DOLIT
 .DW  ')'
 RCALL PARSE
 RJMP TYPES
```

PARSE	Scan the input stream in the Terminal Input Buffer from where >IN points to, until the end of the buffer, for a string delimited by character c. It returns the address and length of the string parsed out. PARSE calls parse to do the detailed works. PARSE is used to implement many specialized parsing commands to perform different parsing functions.
.(	Print the following string till the next) character. It is used to output text to the serial output device.

```
; ( ( -- )
; Ignore following string up to next ) .
; A comment.

 COLON IMEDD+1,"(" PAREN:
 RCALL DOLIT
```

```
 .DW ')'
 RCALL PARSE  RJMP DDROP

;  \ ( -- )
; Ignore following text till the end of line.

 COLON IMEDD+1,"\\"
BKSLA:
 RCALL DOLIT
 .DW  $D
 RCALL PARSE
 RJMP DDROP



;   CHAR ( -- c )
; Parse next word and return its
; first character.

 COLON 4,"CHAR"
CHARR:
 RCALL BLANK
 RCALL PARSE
 RCALL DROP
 RJMP CAT

;   TOKEN ( -- a ; <string> )
; Parse a word from input stream
; and copy it to name dictionary.

; COLON 5,"TOKEN" TOKEN:
 RCALL BLANK
 RCALL PARSE
 RCALL DOLIT
 .DW  31
 RCALL MIN
 RCALL HEREE
```

```
 RCALL  DDUP
 RCALL CSTOR
 RCALL  DDUP
 RCALL PLUS
 ADIW TOSL,1
 RCALL DOLIT
 .DW  0
 RCALL SWAPP
 RCALL CSTOR
 ADIW TOSL,1
 RCALL SWAPP
 RCALL UMOVE
 RJMP HEREE

;   WORD ( c -- a ; <string> )
; Parse a word from input stream
; and copy it to code dictionary.

 COLON 4,"WORD"
WORDD:
 RCALL PARSE
 RCALL HEREE
 RCALL  DDUP

 RCALL CSTOR
 RCALL  DDUP
 RCALL PLUS
 ADIW TOSL,1
 RCALL DOLIT
 .DW  0
 RCALL SWAPP
 RCALL CSTOR
 ADIW TOSL,1
 RCALL SWAPP
 RCALL CMOVE
 RJMP HEREE
```

(	Discard the following string till the next) character. It is used to place comments in source code.
\	Discard all characters till end of a line. It is used to insert comment lines in source code.

CHAR	Parse the next string out but returns only the first character in this string. It gets an ASCII character from the input stream.
TOKEN	Parse out the next string delimited by the space character. It then copies this string as a counted string to the first free area in RAM memory and returns its address. The length of the string is limited to 31 characters.
WORD	Parse out the next string delimited by the ASCII character c. It then copies this string as a counted string to the first free area in RAM memory and returns its address. The length of the string is limited to 255 characters.

5.3.5 Dictionary Search

In 328eForth, command records are linearly linked into a dictionary. A command record contains three fields: a link field holding the name field address of the previous command record, a name field holding the name as a counted string, and a code field holding executable code and data. A dictionary search follows the linked list of records to find a name which matches a text string. It returns the name field address and the code field address, if a match is found.

The link field of the first command record contains a 0, indicating it is the end of the linked list. A system variable CONTEXT holds an address pointing to the name field of the last command record. The dictionary search starts at CONTEXT and terminates at the first matched name, or at the first command record.

From CONTEXT, we locate the name field of the last command record in the dictionary. It this name does not match the string to be searched, we can find the link field of this record, which is 2 bytes less than the name field address. From the link field, we locate the name field of the next command record. Compare the name with the search string. And so forth.

```
 ;; Dictionary search

;   NAME> ( na -- ca )
; Return a code address given a name address.

 COLON 5,"NAME>"
NAMET:
 RCALL ICOUNT
 RCALL DOLIT
 .DW  $1F
 RCALL ANDD
 RCALL PLUS
 RJMP ALGND

;   SAME? ( b a u -- b a f \ -0+ )
; Compare u bytes in two strings.
; Return 0 if identical.

; COLON 5,"SAME?" SAMEQ:
 RCALL TWOSL
 RCALL TOR
 RJMP SAME2
SAME1:
 RCALL OVER
 RCALL RAT
 RCALL CELLS
 RCALL PLUS
 RCALL AT
 RCALL OVER
 RCALL RAT
 RCALL CELLS
 RCALL PLUS
 RCALL IAT
 RCALL SUBB
 RCALL QDUP
 RCALL QBRAN
 .DW  SAME2
 RCALL RFROM
 RJMP DROP
SAME2:
 RCALL DONXT
 .DW  SAME1
 RCALL DOLIT
 .DW  0
 RET
```

NAME>	Convert a name field address in a command record to the code field address of this command record. Code field address is the name field address plus length of name plus one, and aligned to the next cell boundary.
SAME?	Compare two strings at addresses a and b for u bytes. It returns a 0 if two strings are equal. It returns a positive integer if a string is greater than b string. It returns a negative integer if a string is less than b string.

```
;  find ( a va -- ca na | a F )

; Search a vocabulary for a string.
; Return ca and na if succeeded.

; COLON 4,"find"
FIND:
 RCALL SWAPP
 RCALL DUPP
 RCALL CAT
 RCALL TEMP
 RCALL STORE
 RCALL DUPP
 RCALL AT
 RCALL TOR
 ADIW TOSL,2 ;va a+2 --
 RCALL SWAPP ;a+2 va --
FIND1:
 RCALL DUPP
 RCALL QBRAN
 .DW  FIND6
 RCALL DUPP
 RCALL IAT
 RCALL DOLIT
 .DW  $FF3F
 RCALL ANDD
 RCALL RAT
 RCALL XORR
 RCALL QBRAN
```

```
 .DW  FIND2
 ADIW TOSL,2 ;a+2 va+2 --
 RCALL DOLIT
 .DW  -1
 RJMP FIND3
FIND2:
 ADIW TOSL,2 ;a+2 va+2 --
 RCALL TEMP
 RCALL AT
 RCALL SAMEQ
FIND3:
 RJMP FIND4
FIND6:
 RCALL RFROM
 RCALL DROP
 RCALL SWAPP
 SBIW TOSL,2
 RJMP SWAPP
FIND4:
 RCALL QBRAN
 .DW  FIND5
 SBIW TOSL,4
 RCALL IAT
 RJMP FIND1

FIND5:
 RCALL RFROM
 RCALL DROP
 RCALL SWAPP
 RCALL DROP
 SBIW TOSL,2
 RCALL DUPP

 RCALL NAMET
 RJMP SWAPP
```

```
;   NAME? ( a -- ca na | a F )
; Search all context vocabularies
; for a string.

; COLON 5,"NAME?" NAMEQ:
 RCALL CNTXT
 RCALL AT
 RJMP FIND
```

find	Assume that A count string is at RAM memory address a, and the name field address of the last command record is in RAM address va. If the string matches the name of a command, both the code field address and the name field address of the command record are returned. If the string is not a valid command, the original string address and a false flag are returned. find runs the dictionary search very quickly because it first compares the length byte and the first character in the name field as a 16 bit integer. In most cases of mismatch, this comparison would fail and the next record can be reached through the link field. If the first two characters match, then SAME? is invoked to compare the rest of the name field, one cell at a time. Since both the target text string and the name field are null filled to the cell boundary, the comparison can be performed quickly across the entire name field without worrying about the end conditions.
NAME?	Search the dictionary starting at CONTEXT for a name string at address a. Return the code field address and name field address if a matched command is found. Otherwise, return the original string address a and a false flag.

5.3.6 Terminal Input

The text interpreter interprets source text received from an input device and stored in the Terminal Input Buffer. To process characters in the Terminal Input Buffer, we need special commands to deal with the special conditions of backspace character and carriage return: On top of stack, three special parameters are referenced in many commands: bot is the Beginning Of the input Buffer, eot is the End Of the input Buffer, and cur points to the current character in the input buffer.

```
;; Terminal response

;  ^H ( bot eot cur -- bot eot cur )
; Backup the cursor by one character.

; COLON 2,"^H"
BKSP:
 RCALL TOR
 RCALL OVER
 RCALL RFROM
 RCALL SWAPP
```

```
RCALL OVER
 RCALL XORR
 RCALL QBRAN
 .DW  BACK1
 RCALL DOLIT
 .DW  BKSPP
 RCALL EMIT
 SBIW TOSL,1
 RCALL BLANK
 RCALL EMIT
 RCALL DOLIT
 .DW  BKSPP
 RCALL EMIT
BACK1:
 RET

;  TAP ( bot eot cur c -- bot eot cur )
; Accept and echo the key stroke
; and bump the cursor.
```

```
; COLON 3,"TAP"
TAP:
 RCALL DUPP
 RCALL EMIT
 RCALL OVER
 RCALL CSTOR
 adiw tosl,1
 ret

;   kTAP ( bot eot cur c -- bot eot cur )
; Process a key stroke, CR or backspace.

; COLON 4,"kTAP" K
TAP:
 RCALL DUPP
 SBIW TOSL,CRR
 RCALL QBRAN
 .DW  KTAP2
 SBIW TOSL,BKSPP
 RCALL QBRAN
 .DW  KTAP1
 RCALL BLANK
 RJMP TAP
KTAP1:
 RJMP BKSP
KTAP2:
 RCALL DROP
 RCALL SWAPP
 RCALL DROP
 RJMP DUPP

;   accept ( b u -- b u )
; Accept characters to input buffer.
; Return with actual count.

; COLON 6,"accept"
ACCEP:
 RCALL OVER
 RCALL PLUS
 RCALL OVER
ACCP1:
 RCALL DDUP
 RCALL XORR
 RCALL QBRAN
 .DW  ACCP4
```

```
 RCALL KEY
 RCALL DUPP
 RCALL BLANK
 RCALL SUBB
 RCALL DOLIT
 .DW $5F
 RCALL ULESS
 RCALL QBRAN
 .DW ACCP2
 RCALL TAP
 RJMP ACCP3
ACCP2:
 RCALL KTAP
ACCP3:
 RJMP ACCP1
ACCP4:
 RCALL DROP
 RCALL OVER
 RJMP SUBB
```

^H	Process back-space character (ASCII 8). It erases the last character entered, and decrement the character pointer cur. If cur=bot, do nothing because you cannot backup beyond beginning of input buffer.
TAP	Output a character c to terminal, store c in cur, and increment the character pointer cur, which points to the current character in the input buffer. bot and eot are also pointers pointing to the beginning and end of the input buffer.
kTAP	Process character c. bot is pointing at the beginning of the input buffer, and eot is pointing at the end. cur points to the current character in the input buffer. The character c is normally stored at cur, which is then incremented by 1. If c is a carriage-return (ASCII 13), echo a space and make eot=cur., thus terminating the input process If c is a back-space (ASCII 8), erase the last character and decrement cur.

accept	Accept u characters into an input buffer starting at address b, or until a carriage return (ASCII 13) is encountered. The value of u returned is the actual number of characters received.

```
;  EXPECT ( b u -- )
; Accept input stream and store count in SPAN.

 COLON 6,"EXPECT"
EXPEC:
 RCALL ACCEP
 RCALL SPAN
 RCALL STORE
 RJMP DROP
```

```
;  QUERY ( -- )
; Accept input stream to terminal
; input buffer.

 COLON 5,"QUERY"
QUERY:
 RCALL TIB
 RCALL DOLIT
 .DW  80
 RCALL ACCEP
 RCALL NTIB
 RCALL STORE
 RCALL DROP
 RCALL DOLIT
 .DW  0
 RCALL INN
 RJMP STORE
```

EXPECT	Accept u characters into an input buffer starting at b, or until a carriage return is encountered. The number of characters received is stored in system variable SPAN.
QUERY	Accept up to 80 characters from the input device to the Terminal Input Buffer. It also prepares the Terminal Input Buffer for parsing by setting #TIB to the length of the input text stream, and clearing >IN which points to the beginning of the Terminal Input Buffer.

5.4 Interpreter

5.4.1 Error Handling

When error occurred, it is usually because the text interpreter encounters a string which can not be interpreted or processed. This string is usually stored in a buffer in RAM memory.

```
;; Error handling


;   ERROR ( a -- )
; Return address of a null string
; with zero count.

; COLON 5,"ERROR" ERROR:
 RCALL SPACE
 RCALL COUNT
 RCALL TYPES
 RCALL DOLIT
 .DW  $3F
 RCALL EMIT
 RCALL CR
 RCALL EMPTY_BUF
 ldi  yl,low(SPP)
 ldi  yh,high(SPP)
 RJMP QUIT
```

```
; abort" ( f -- )
; Run time routine of ABORT" .
; Abort with a message.

; COLON COMPO+6,"abort"
; .DB ''''
ABORQ:
 RCALL QBRAN
 .DW ABOR1 ;text flag
 RCALL DOSTR
 RCALL ICOUNT ;pass error string
 RCALL ITYPES
 RCALL CR
 RJMP QUIT
ABOR1:
 RCALL DOSTR
 RJMP DROP
```

ERROR	Print the string in RAM memory located at address a, followed by a ? mark and aborts. 'Abort' means flushing all flash memory buffers, clearing the parameter stack, and returns to the text interpreter loop QUIT.
abort"	It is compiled with an error message string in a compound command. When abort" is executed, it examines the top item on the parameter stack. It the flag is true, print out the following error message and QUIT; otherwise, skip over the error message and continue execution the next token.

5.4.2 Interpreter

Text interpreter in FORTH is like a conventional operating system of a computer. It is the primary interface a user uses to get the computer to do work. Since FORTH uses very simple syntax rule--commands are separated by spaces, the text interpreter is also very simple. It accepts a line of text from the terminal, parses out a command delimited by spaces, locates the command in the dictionary and then executes it. The process is repeated until the input text is exhausted. Then the text interpreter waits for another line of text and interprets it again. This cycle repeats until you are exhausted and turns off the computer.

In 328eForth, the text interpreter is coded as the command QUIT. QUIT contains an infinite loop which repeats the QUERY-EVAL command pair. QUERY accepts a line of text from the input terminal. EVAL interprets the text one command at a time till the end of the text line.

```
;; The text interpreter

;  $INTERPRET ( a -- )
; Interpret a word. If failed,
; try to convert it to an integer.

; COLON 10,"$INTERPRET" INTER:
 RCALL NAMEQ
 RCALL QDUP ;?defined
```

```
 RCALL QBRAN
 .DW  INTE1
 RCALL IAT
 RCALL DOLIT
 .DW  COMPO
 RCALL ANDD ;?compile only lexicon bits
 RCALL ABORQ
 .DB  13," compile only"
 RCALL EXECU
 RET ;execute defined word INTE1:
 RCALL NUMBQ
 RCALL QBRAN
 .DW  INTE2
 RET
INTE2:
 RJMP ERROR ;error

;  [ ( -- )
; Start the text interpreter.

 COLON IMEDD+1,"[" LBRAC:
 RCALL DOLIT
 .DW  INTER*2
 RCALL TEVAL  RJMP STORE
```

```
; .OK ( -- )
; Display "ok" only while interpreting.

; COLON 3,".OK" DOTOK:
 RCALL DOLIT
 .DW INTER*2
 RCALL TEVAL
 RCALL AT
 RCALL EQUAL
 RCALL QBRAN
 .DW DOTO1
 RCALL DOTQP
 .DB 2,"ok"
DOTO1:
RJMP CR
```

$INTERPRET	Execute a command whose name string is stored at address a on the parameter stack. If the string is not a valid command, convert it to a number. Failing the numeric conversion, execute ERROR and return to QUIT.
[	Activate the text interpreter by storing the code field address of $INTERPRET into the variable 'EVAL, which is executed in EVAL while the text interpreter is in the interpretive mode.
.OK	Print the familiar ok> prompting message after executing to the end of a line. The message ok> is printed only when the text interpreter is in the interpretive mode. While compiling, the prompt is suppressed.

```
; ?STACK ( -- )
; Abort if the data stack underflows.

; COLON 6,"?STACK" QSTAC:
 RCALL DEPTH
 RCALL ZLESS ;check only for underflow
 RCALL ABORQ
```

```
 .DB  10," underflow"
 RET

;   EVAL ( -- )
; Interpret the input stream.

; COLON 4,"EVAL" EVAL:
EVAL1: RCALL TOKEN
 RCALL DUPP
 RCALL CAT   ;?input stream empty
 RCALL QBRAN
 .DW  EVAL2
 RCALL TEVAL
 RCALL ATEXE ;
 RCALL INTER
 RCALL QSTAC ;evaluate input, check stack
 RJMP EVAL1
EVAL2:
 RCALL DROP
 RJMP DOTOK

;; Shell

;   QUIT ( -- )
; Reset return stack pointer and
; start text interpreter.

 COLON 4,"QUIT"
QUIT:
 ldi  xl,low(RPP)
 out_  SPL,xl
 ldi  xh,high(RPP)
 out_  SPH,xh
 RCALL DOLIT
 .DW  TIBB
 RCALL TTIB
 RCALL STORE
QUIT1:
 RCALL LBRAC ;start interpretation
QUIT2:
 RCALL QUERY ;get input
 RCALL EVAL
 RJMP QUIT2 ;continue till error
```

?STACK	Check for stack underflow. Abort, resetting the parameter stack pointer,
	if the stack depth is negative.
EVAL	It is contained in the text interpreter loop which parses commands from the input stream and invokes whatever token in 'EVAL to process the commands, either execute it with $INTERPRET or compile it with $COMPILE.
QUIT	It is the operating system, the text interpreter, or a shell, of the 328eForth system. It is an infinite loop eForth will never get out. It uses QUERY to accept a line of commands from the input terminal and then lets EVAL to parse out the commands and execute them. After a line is processed, it displays an ok> message and wait for the next line of commands. When an error occurred during execution, it prints the string which caused the error as an error message. After the error is reported, it re-initializes the system by clearing the return stack and comes back to receive the next line of commands. Because the behavior of EVAL can be changed by storing either $INTERPRET or $COMPILE into 'EVAL, QUIT exhibits the dual nature of a text interpreter and a compiler.

5.4.3 Tools

328eForth is a very small system and only a very small set of tool commands are provided. Nevertheless, this set of tool commands is powerful enough to help you debug new commands he adds to the system. They are also very interesting programming examples on how to use the commands in eForth to build applications.

Generally, the tool commands present information stored in different parts of the CPU in appropriate formats to let you inspect the results as he executes commands in the eForth system and commands he defined himself. The tool commands include memory dump, stack dump, dictionary dump, etc.

```
;  '( -- ca )
; Search context vocabularies for the next
; word in input stream.

 COLON 1,"'"
 TICK:
 RCALL TOKEN
 RCALL NAMEQ ;?defined
 RCALL QBRAN
 .DW  TICK1
 RET    ;yes, push code address
TICK1:
 RJMP ERROR ;no, error

 ;; Tools

;   DUMP ( a -- )
; Dump 128 bytes from a, in a
; formatted manner.
 COLON 4,"DUMP"
 DUMP:
 RCALL DOLIT
 .DW  7
 RCALL TOR  ;start count down loop
DUMP1: RCALL CR
 RCALL DUPP
 RCALL DOLIT
 .DW  5
 RCALL UDOTR
 RCALL SPACE
 RCALL DOLIT
 .DW  15
 RCALL TOR
DUMP2:
 RCALL COUNT
 RCALL DOLIT
 .DW  3
 RCALL UDOTR
 RCALL DONXT ;display printable characters
 .DW  DUMP2
 RCALL SPACE
 RCALL DUPP
 RCALL DOLIT
 .DW  16
```

```
RCALL SUBB
RCALL DOLIT
 .DW  16
RCALL TYPES
RCALL DONXT
.DW  DUMP1 ;loop till done
RJMP DROP
```

'	Search the dictionary for the following string. If the string is a valid command, return its code field address. If the string is not a valid command, print a ? mark.
DUMP	Print 128 bytes of data starting at RAM address b to the terminal. It dumps 16 bytes to a line. A line begins with the address of the first byte, followed by 16 bytes shown in hex, 3 columns per bytes. At the end of a line are the 16 bytes shown in ASCII characters. Non-printable characters are replaced by underscores (ASCII 95). ATmega328P has memory organized in 128 byte pages. It is convenient to dump memory one page at a time. DUMP commands in most FORTH system takes and address and a length as parameters to dump a memory array.

```
 ;  IDUMP ( a -- )
; Dump u bytes from a, in a formatted manner.

 COLON 5,"IDUMP"
IDUMP:
 RCALL DOLIT
 .DW  7
 RCALL TOR  ;start count down loop IDUMP1:
 RCALL CR
 RCALL DUPP
 RCALL DOLIT
 .DW  5
 RCALL UDOTR
 RCALL SPACE
 RCALL DOLIT
 .DW  15  RCALL TOR
```

```
IDUMP2:
 RCALL ICOUNT
 RCALL DOLIT .DW 3
 RCALL UDOTR
 RCALL DONXT ;display printable characters
 .DW IDUMP2
 RCALL SPACE  RCALL DUPP
 RCALL DOLIT
 .DW 16
 RCALL SUBB
 RCALL DOLIT
 .DW 16
 RCALL ITYPES
 RCALL DONXT
 .DW IDUMP1 ;loop till done
 RJMP DROP


; .S ( ... -- ... )
; Display the contents of the data stack.

 COLON 2,".S"
DOTS:
 RCALL DEPTH ;stack depth
 RCALL TOR ;start count down loop
 RJMP  DOTS2  ;skip  first  pass
DOTS1:
 RCALL RAT
 RCALL PICK
 RCALL DOT ;index stack, display contents DOTS2:
 RCALL DONXT
 .DW DOTS1 ;loop till done
 RCALL DOTQP
 .DB 4," <sp"
 RET
```

IDUMP	Print 128 bytes of data starting at flash address a to the terminal. It dumps 16 bytes to a line. A line begins with the address of the first byte, followed by 16 bytes shown in hex, 3 columns per bytes. At the end of a line are the 16 bytes shown in ASCII characters. Non-printable characters are replaced by underscores (ASCII 95). ATmega328P organizes the flash memory in pages of 128 bytes. It is convenient to dump flash memory one page at a time. ATmega328P uses 16-bit machine instructions, and addresses flash memory using 16-bit cell addresses. I choose to address flash memory also in bytes, and IDUMP displays byte addresses. Be aware of this difference when you read machine instructions.

One important discipline in learning FORTH is to learn how to use the parameter stack effectively. All commands must consume their input parameters on the stack and leave only their intended results on the stack. Sloppy usage of the parameter stack is often the cause of bugs which are very difficult to detect later, as unexpected items left on the stack could result in unpredictable behavior. .S should be used liberally during programming and debugging to ensure that the correct parameters are left on the parameter stack.

The parameter stack is the center for arithmetic and logic operations. It is where commands receive their parameters and also where they left their results. In debugging a new command which may use stack items and leave items on the stack, the best was to debug it is to inspect the parameter stack, before and after its execution. To inspect the parameter stack non-destructively, use the command .S.

.S	Print the contents of the parameter stack in the free format. The bottom of the stack is aligned to the left margin. The top item is shown towards the left and followed by the characters <sp. .S does not change the data stack so it can be used to inspect the data stack non-destructively at any time.

The dictionary contains all command records defined in the system, ready for execution and compilation. WORDS command allows you to examine the dictionary and to look for the correct names of commands in case you are not sure of their spellings. WORDS follows the dictionary link in the system variable CONTEXT and displays the names of all commands in the dictionary. The dictionary links can be traced easily because the link field in the header of a command points to the name field of the previous command, and the link field is two bytes below the corresponding name field.

>NAME finds the name field address of a word from the corresponding code field address in a command record. If the command does not exist in the dictionary, it returns a false flag. It is the mirror image of the command NAME>, which returns the code field address of a command from its name field address. It is difficult to scan backward from code field to locate the beginning of the name field, because we do not know how long the name field is. >NAME is therefore more complicated because the entire dictionary must be searched to locate its name field.

```
;  >NAME ( ca -- na | F )
; Convert code address to a name address.

; COLON 5,">NAME" TNAME:
 RCALL TOR
 RCALL CNTXT
 RCALL AT ;na
TNAM1:
 RCALL DUPP ;na na
 RCALL QBRAN
 .DW  TNAM2
 RCALL DUPP  ;na na
 RCALL NAMET ;na ca
 RCALL RAT   ;na ca ca
 RCALL XORR  ;na f
 RCALL QBRAN
 .DW  TNAM2
 SBIW TOSL,2  ;la
 RCALL IAT    ;na'
 RCALL BRAN
 .DW  TNAM1
TNAM2:
 RCALL RFROM ;na or 0
 RJMP DROP

;  .ID ( na -- )
; Display the name at address.
```

```
; COLON 3,".ID" DOTID:
 RCALL ICOUNT
 RCALL DOLIT
 .DW 31
 RCALL ANDD
 RJMP ITYPES

; WORDS ( -- )
; Display the names in the context vocabulary.

 COLON 5,"WORDS"
WORDS:
 RCALL CR
 RCALL CNTXT
 RCALL AT ;na
WORS1:
 RCALL QDUP  ;end of list?
 RCALL QBRAN
 .DW WORS2
 RCALL DUPP  ;na na
 RCALL SPACE
 RCALL DOTID ;display a name
 SBIW TOSL,2 ;la
 RCALL IAT   ;na'
 RCALL BRAN
 .DW WORS1
WORS2:
 RET
```

>NAME	Return a code field address, xt, of a command from its name field address, na. If xt is not a valid code field address, return 0. It follows the linked list of the dictionary, and from every name field address we can get a corresponding code field address. If this address is not the same as xt, we go to the name field of the next command. If xt is a valid code field address, we surely will find it. If the entire dictionary is searched and xt is not found, it is not a valid code field address.
.ID	Display the name of a command, given the name field address of this command. It replaces non-printable characters in a name by

	under-scores.
WORDS	Display all the names in the dictionary. The order of words is reversed from the compiled order. The last defined command is shown first.

5.4.4 Startup

After the computer is turned on, it executes some native machine code at START to set up the CPU hardware. Then it jumps to COLD to initialize the 328eForth system which is the FORTH Virtual Machine. It finally jumps to QUIT and starts the text interpreter. COLD and QUIT are the topmost layers of 328eForth system.

Because all the system variable in 328eForth are initialized from a data array in flash memory, 328eForth is eminently ROMable and suitable for embedded applications in ATmega328P. Before falling into QUIT to enter into the text interpreter loop, COLD command executes a boot routine whose code address is stored in system variable 'BOOT. This code address can be vectored to an application command which defines the proper behavior of the system on power-up and on reset. Initially 'BOOT contains the code field address of hi.

```
;; Hardware reset

;  hi ( -- )
; Display the sign-on message of eForth.

; COLON 2,"hi"
HI:
; RCALL STOIO
 RCALL CR
 RCALL DOTQP  ;initialize I/O
 .DB  15,"328eForth v3.01" ;model
 RJMP CR

;  COLD ( -- )
; The hilevel cold start sequence.

 COLON 4,"COLD"
COLD:
```

```
COLD1:
 RCALL STOIO
 RCALL DOLIT
 .DW  $100
 RCALL DUPP
 RCALL READ ;initialize user area
 RCALL DOLIT ;init older buffer
 .DW  OLDER
 RCALL AT  ;
 RCALL READ_FLASH
 RCALL SWITCH
 RCALL DOLIT ;init newer buffer
 .DW  OLDER
 RCALL AT  ;
 RCALL READ_FLASH
 RCALL SWITCH
 RCALL DDROP
 RCALL TBOOT
 RCALL ATEXE
 RJMP QUIT ;start interpretation
```

hi	The default start-up routine in 328eForth. It initializes the serial I/O device and then displays a sign-on message. This is where you can customize his application. From here one can initialize the system to start his own application.
'BOOT	A system variable loaded at RAM memory address $100. It is originally vectored to hi.
COLD	A high level compound command executed upon power-up, called from the low level START routine. Its initializes the system variables, executes the boot-up routine vectored through 'BOOT, and then falls into the text interpreter loop QUIT.

5.5 Compiler

ATmega328P, with its Harvard architecture, is very hostile to FORTH. It is difficult to extend an interactive FORTH system in the flash memory. You can change erased bits from 1 to 0. But, when you want to change bit 0 to bit 1, you have to erase a whole page. The flash memory in ATmega328P is specified to endure 10,000 erase cycles. You have to be very careful about these erase cycles when you are programming in FORTH, because you will write and re-write many small commands many, many times until you get them right. To minimize the erase cycles and to extend the life of flash memory, I took out the big gun in Chuck Moore's arsenal: the ping-pong BLOCK buffers.

I use two 128 byte page buffers to store compiled code. New FORTH commands are compiled into these buffers. Two buffers are necessary so that forward references can be resolved across a page boundary. Otherwise, many more erase cycles would be wasted when building structures in adjacent pages of flash memory. Only when both buffers are full, the least recently used buffer is flushed into the flash memory, before a new page of flash memory is read into this buffer.

The disadvantage is that after a new command is defined, you cannot execute it unless it is first flushed. Executing a command in a buffer will definitely crash the system. Always remember to include a FLUSH command at the end of a source code file. When you are compiling lines of code interactively, remember to do a FLUSH before executing any command you just typed in. Otherwise, be prepared for a crash and reload 328eForth system from AVR Studio 4. This error will happen, believe me, and it is distressing. But, remember we are dealing with a microcontroller, and its flash memory can endure only 10,000 erase cycles.

5.5.1 Access Flash Memory

```
; Flash memory read, write, and erase.

.equ PAGESIZEB = PAGESIZE*2 ;PAGESIZEB
; is page size in BYTES, not words
.def spmcrval = r20
.def looplo = r22
.def loophi = r23
```

```
; Page Erase
; ERASE ( a -- )
; Erase a page of flash memory

 COLON 5,"ERASE"
ERASE:
 movw zl,tosl
 loadtos
ERASE_1:
 ldi  spmcrval, (1<<PGERS) | (1<<SELFPRGEN)
 rcall  Do_spm
; re-enable the RWW section
 ldi  spmcrval, (1<<RWWSRE) |
          (1<<SELFPRGEN)
 rjmp  Do_spm

; Page Write
;  WRITE ( ram flash -- )
;  transfer data from RAM to
;  Flash page buffer

 COLON 5,"WRITE"
WRITE:
 movw zl, tosl
 loadtos
 movw xl, tosl
 loadtos
WRITE_1:
 ldi  looplo, low(PAGESIZEB) ;init loop
                         ; variable Wrloop:
 ld   r0, X+
 ld   r1, X+
 ldi  spmcrval, (1<<SELFPRGEN)
 rcall  Do_spm
 adiw  ZL, 2
 subi  looplo, 2 ;use subi for PAGESIZEB<=256
 brne  Wrloop
; execute Page Write
 subi  ZL, low(PAGESIZEB)  ;restore pointer
 sbci  ZH, high(PAGESIZEB) ;not required
                        ; for PAGESIZEB<=256
 ldi  spmcrval, (1<<PGWRT) | (1<<SELFPRGEN)
 rcall  Do_spm  ; re-enable the RWW section
 ldi  spmcrval, (1<<RWWSRE) | (1<<SELFPRGEN)
```

```
 rjmp  Do_spm

; Page Read
;  READ ( flash ram -- )
;  transfer data from Flash to RAM page buffer

 COLON 4,"READ"
READ:
 movw xl,tosl
 loadtos
```

```
 movw zl,tosl  loadtos
READ_1:
; read back and check, optional
 ldi  looplo, low(PAGESIZEB)   ;init loop
                          ; variable Rdloop:
 lpm  r0, Z+
 st   X+, r0
 subi  looplo, 1 ;use subi for PAGESIZEB<=256
 brne  Rdloop
 ret

Do_spm:
; check for previous SPM complete Wait_spm:
 in   temp1, SPMCSR
 sbrc  temp1, SELFPRGEN
 rjmp  Wait_spm
; SPM timed sequence
 out  SPMCSR,
 spmcrval  spm
 ret
```

ERASE	Erase one 128 byte page of flash memory. The page address a is on the top of the parameter stack.
WRITE	Copy the contents of one 128 byte page in RAM memory, starting at RAM address ram, to an page of flash memory, starting at flash address flash. All addresses are byte addresses.

READ	Copy the contents of one 128 byte page in flash memory, starting at flash address flash, to an page of RAM memory, starting at RAM address ram. All addresses are byte addresses.

ERASE, WRITE, and READ commands are all adapted from sample code listed in the AVR Data Book published by Atmel Corp: doc8271.pdf, "8-Bit AVR Microcontroller with 4/8/16/32K Bytes In-System Programmable Flash".

5.5.2 Buffers and Pointers

To 128-byte buffers are allocated in the high end of RAM memory: BUF0 at $800, and BUF1 at $880, for flash memory accessing. Two buffer pointers are allocated at low RAM memory: NEW at $11C and OLD at $1E. The buffer pointers have the following format:

15	Bits14-7	Bits 6-1	0
Dirty Bit	Page Address	Byte Address	Buffer Code

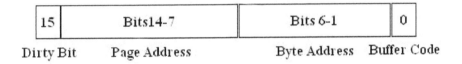

Format of Flash Buffer Pointer

The buffer pointer actually hold the address of a byte in flash memory. Bits 14-7 are for the page address, and bits 6-0 are byte address within a page. Since ATmega328P has only 32 KB of flash memory, Bit 15 is not used for addressing, and is reserved for a Dirty Bit which indicates whether the contents in this buffer was modified. If Dirty Bit is set, its contents must be flushed back into the flash memory when this buffer is allocated for another page of flash memory. If this Dirty Bit is cleared, the buffer has not been modified, and another page can be loaded into this buffer immediately.

As flash memory is accessed one page at a time, the Byte Address field is always cleared. The least significant Bit 0 is used to determine which physical buffer is associated with this buffer pointer. Bit 0 is cleared when the buffer pointer points to BUF0 at $800. Bit 0 is set when the buffer pointer points to BUF1 at $880.

Buffer pointer NEW at $11C always points to the buffer which is most recently accessed, and buffer pointer OLD at $11E always points to the buffer with is accessed earlier. When we need to access a new page of flash memory, it is always read into the buffer pointed to by OLD. If data in OLD was modified and its Dirty Bit is set, data in the old buffer must be flushed to flash memory before a new page of data is read in.

```
;  I@ ( a -- w )
; Push flash memory cell to the data stack.
 CODE 2,"I@"
IAT:
 RCALL DOLIT  .DW  NEWER
 RCALL BUFQ ;n a new?
 RCALL QBRAN ;if a=new, fetch n in new_buf
 .DW  IAT1 ;else, a=old?
 RCALL DOLIT ;n a a old
 .DW  OLDER
 RCALL BUFQ ;n a old?
 RCALL QBRAN ;if a=old, fetch n in old_buf
 .DW  IAT2
 movw  zl, tosl ;else, fetch from flash
 lpm  tosl, z+  lpm  tosh, z+
 RET
IAT1:
 RCALL DOLIT
 .DW  NEWER
 RJMP IAT3
IAT2:
 RCALL DOLIT
 .DW  OLDER
IAT3:
 RCALL BUFAT
 RJMP AT


;  IC@ ( a -- w )
; Push flash memory byte to the data stack.
 CODE 3,"IC@"
```

```
ICAT:
 RCALL DOLIT
```

```
 .DW  NEWER
 RCALL BUFQ ;n a new?
 RCALL QBRAN ;if a=new, fetch n in new_buf
 .DW  ICAT1 ;else, a=old?
 RCALL DOLIT ;n a a old
 .DW  OLDER
 RCALL BUFQ ;n a old?
 RCALL QBRAN ;if a=old, fetch n in old_buf
 .DW  ICAT2
 movw  zl, tosl ;else, fetch from flash
 clr  tosh  lpm  tosl, Z
 RET
ICAT1:
 RCALL DOLIT
 .DW  NEWER
 RJMP ICAT3
ICAT2:
 RCALL DOLIT
 .DW  OLDER
ICAT3:
 RCALL BUFAT
 RJMP CAT
```

I@	Fetch 16 bit data from a flash cell memory, whose byte address a is on the top of the parameter stack. It first sees if this data is in the NEW flash buffer. If true, fetch data from NEW buffer. If not true, it then sees if this data is in the OLD buffer. If true, fetch data from OLD buffer, and also switch NEW and OLD buffers. If no true, data is in flash memory, and fetch it from flash memory directly. Cell memory address a is a byte address.
IC@	Fetch 8 bit data from flash memory, whose byte address a is on the top of the parameter stack. It first sees if this data is in the NEW flash buffer. If true, fetch data from NEW buffer. If not true, it then sees if this data is in the OLD buffer. If true, fetch data from OLD buffer, and also switch NEW and OLD buffers. If no true, data is in flash memory, and fetch it from flash memory directly.

```
; CODE 6,"BUFFER" ; ptr -- buf BUFFER:
 RCALL DOLIT
 .DW  $1
 RCALL ANDD
 RCALL QBRAN
 .DW  BUF_1
 RCALL DOLIT
 .DW  BUF1
 RET
BUF_1:
 RCALL DOLIT
 .DW  BUF0
 RET

; CODE 6,"BUF?" ; a new/old -- f BUFQ:
 RCALL AT
 RCALL OVER
 RCALL XORR
 RCALL DOLIT
 .DW  $7F80
 RCALL ANDD
 RET

; CODE 6,"BUF@" ; a new/old -- buf_addr BUFAT:
 RCALL AT
 RCALL BUFFER
 RCALL SWAPP
 RCALL DOLIT
 .DW  $7F
 RCALL ANDD
 RJMP XORR
```

BUFFER	Convert a buffer pointer ptr to the address of the flash buffer buf, associated with the buffer pointer.
BUF?	Determine whether the data at address a is inside the buffer whose pointer new/old is on the top of the parameter stack. It compares Bits 14-7 in the address and in the buffer pointer.
BUF@	Convert the flash memory address a to the corresponding address in the buffer pointed to by the buffer pointer new/old on the top of the parameter stack.

```
; I! ( w a -- )
; Store w to flash memory byte location.

 CODE 2,"I!"
ISTOR:   ;a=new?
 RCALL DOLIT
 .DW  NEWER
 RCALL BUFQ ;n a a new_ptr
 RCALL QBRAN ;if a=new, store n in new_buf
 .DW  ISTOR5 ;else, a=old?
;
 RCALL DOLIT ;n a a old
 .DW  OLDER
 RCALL BUFQ   ; n a a old_ptr
 RCALL QBRAN  ; if a=old, switch ptrs,
              ; store n in new_buf
 .DW  ISTOR4 ;else, flush old_buf

 RCALL DOLIT ;n a old
 .DW  OLDER
 RCALL AT ;n a old_ptr
 RCALL DOLIT ;n a dirty?
 .DW  $8000
 RCALL ANDD
 RCALL QBRAN ; if not dirty, go read flash
             ; data into old_buf
 .DW  ISTOR2 ;else, flush old_buf to flash

ISTOR1: RCALL FLUSH_OLD
ISTOR2: RCALL READ_FLASH
```

```
ISTOR3: RCALL UPDATE_OLD ISTOR4:
 RCALL SWITCH
ISTOR5: RJMP  UPDATE_NEW

; CODE 5,"FLUSH" ; --
FLUSH_OLD:
 RCALL DOLIT ;old
 .DW  OLDER
 RCALL AT ;old_ptr
 RCALL DUPP ;old_ptr old_ptr
 RCALL DOLIT
 .DW  $7F80
 RCALL ANDD ;old_ptr flash_addr
 RCALL DUPP ;old_ptr flash_addr flash_addr
 RCALL ERASE ;old_ptr flash_addr
;
 RCALL SWAPP  ;flash_addr old_ptr
 RCALL BUFFER ;flash_addr buf
 RCALL SWAPP  ;buf flash_addr
 RJMP WRITE
```

I!	Store the data w in flash memory address a.
FLUSH_OLD	First erase the flash memory page corresponding to the page stored in OLD buffer, and copy contents in the OLD buffer to this page in flash memory.

5.5.3 Write to Flash

I! is the most interesting command in the flash memory command set, and needs a more detailed explanation. Its action follows the follow steps:

1. If the flash page addressed by a is in the NEW buffer, go to step 8.
2. If the flash page addressed by a is in the OLD buffer, go to step 7.
3. If the flash page addressed by a is not in either buffer, test the Dirty Bit in OLD buffer pointer. If the Dirty Bit is not set, go to step 5.
4. OLD buffer is dirty, flush its contents. Continue to step 5.
5. Read the flash memory page pointed to by address a into the OLD buffer.

6. Update OLD buffer pointer with the page address derived from a. Clear the Dirty Bit in OLD buffer pointer.
7. Switch contents in OLD and NEW, so that the OLD buffer becomes the most recently accessed buffer.
8. Write data w into NEW buffer to the address corresponding to a, and set the Dirty Bit in the NEW buffer pointer.

This scheme of data buffering was first used by Chuck Moore in his implementation of virtual memory to access data stored on magnetic tapes and on magnetic disks. He divided all external storage media into blocks of 1024 bytes and manage them with buffers in RAM. His scheme minimized accesses to external media and achieved execution speed unheard of on computers of the earlier eras.

```
; CODE 4,"@OLD" ;a -- a
READ_FLASH: ;read new flash data
            ;into old_buf
 RCALL DOLIT ;a old
 .DW  OLDER
 RCALL AT  ;a old_ptr
 RCALL BUFFER ;a buf
 RCALL OVER ;a buf a
 RCALL DOLIT
 .DW  $7F80
 RCALL ANDD ;a buf flash_addr
 RCALL SWAPP ;a flash_addr buf
 RJMP READ ;a

; CODE 4,"!OLD" ;a --
UPDATE_OLD:  ;preserve buf? bit
 RCALL DUPP ;a a
 RCALL DOLIT ;
 .DW  $7F80
 RCALL ANDD ;a page_addr
 RCALL DOLIT
 .DW  OLDER  ;a page_addr old
 RCALL SWAPP ;a old page_addr
 RCALL OVER  ;a old page_addr old
 RCALL AT    ;a old page_addr old_ptr
 RCALL DOLIT
 .DW  $1
 RCALL ANDD  ;a old page_addr buf?
 RCALL ORR   ;a old updates_old_ptr
```

```
 RCALL SWAPP ;a old_ptr old
 RJMP STORE ;a

; CODE 6,"SWITCH" ; --
SWITCH:
 RCALL DOLIT ;old
 .DW  OLDER
 RCALL AT    ;old_ptr
 RCALL DOLIT ;old_ptr new
 .DW  NEWER
 RCALL AT    ;old_ptr new_ptr
 RCALL DOLIT ;old_ptr new_ptr old
 .DW   OLDER
 RCALL STORE ;old_ptr
 RCALL DOLIT ;old_ptr new
 .DW  NEWER
 RJMP STORE ;

; CODE 4,"!NEW" ;n a --
UPDATE_NEW:   ; write data to new buffer,
              ; set dirty bit
 RCALL DOLIT ;n a 7e
 .DW  $7E
 RCALL ANDD  ;n disp
 RCALL DOLIT ;n disp new
 .DW   NEWER
 RCALL AT    ;n disp new_ptr
 RCALL BUFFER ;n disp buf UPDAT1:
 RCALL ORR   ;n buff_addr
 RCALL STORE  ;update word in new_buf
 RCALL DOLIT  ;set dirty bit in newer
 .DW   NEWER
 RCALL DUPP   ;newer newer
 RCALL AT     ;newer new_ptr
 RCALL DOLIT
 .DW   $8000
 RCALL ORR    ;newer new_ptr_dirty
 RCALL SWAPP
 RJMP STORE   ;new buf is dirty now

; EMPTY-BUFFERS ( -- )
 CODE 5,"FLUSH"

EMPTY_BUF:
```

```
 RCALL EMPTY_OLD
 RCALL SWITCH
 RCALL EMPTY_OLD
 RJMP  SWITCH

; EMPTY_OLD ;flush old buffer
;   if it is dirty

EMPTY_OLD:
 RCALL DOLIT  ;old
 .DW   OLDER
 RCALL AT     ;old_ptr
 RCALL DUPP   ;old_ptr old_ptr
 RCALL DOLIT  ;
 .DW   $8000
 RCALL ANDD   ;old_ptr dirty?
 RCALL QBRAN  ;if not dirty, exit
 .DW  EMPTY_1 ;else, flush old_buf
;
 RCALL DOLIT ;old_ptr
 .DW   $7FFF
 RCALL ANDD  ;old_ptr, dirty bit cleared
 RCALL DOLIT
 .DW  OLDER
 RCALL STORE ;old_ptr flash_addr
 RJMP FLUSH_OLD
EMPTY_1:
 RJMP DROP
```

@OLD	Read one page of the flash memory pointed to a address a into the OLD buffer.
!OLD	Update the OLD buffer pointer so that it now had the page address corresponding to flash memory address a.
SWTICH	Exchange the contents of NEW and OLD buffer pointers, so that the OLD buffer becomes NEW, the most recently accessed buffer.
!NEW	Write new data w into NEW buffer at aa address corresponding to

	flash memory address a. Set Dirty Bit in NEW buffer pointer.
EMPTY_OLD	Flush OLD buffer to flash memory if it is dirty.
FLUSH	Flush both buffers back to flash memory.

5.5.4 Compiler Commands

The bootloader section in the flash memory of ATmega328P has only 4 KB space, which is not enough to host the entire 328eForth system. I only managed to squeeze the text interpreter into the bootloader section. Assembler now continues assembly at flash memory byte address $200. The correct cell address is $100.

```
;=====================================
; Compiler

.org $100

;  1+ ( a -- a )
; Add 1 to address.

 COLON 2,"1+"
ONEP:
 adiw tosl,1
 ret

;  1- ( a -- a )
; Subtract 1 from address.

 COLON 2,"1-"
ONEM:
 sbiw tosl,1  ret



;  2+ ( a -- a )
; Add cell size in byte to address.

 COLON 2,"2+"
CELLP:
 adiw tosl,2
 ret



;  2- ( a -- a )
; Subtract cell size in byte from address.

 COLON 2,"2-"
CELLM:
```

```
sbiw tosl,2
ret

; > ( n1 n2 -- flag ) Compare
; compares two values (signed)

COLON 1,">"
```

```
GREATER:
ld  temp2, Y+ ld  temp3, Y+
cp  temp2,
tosl cpc temp3, tosh rjmp DGRE1

; D> ( d1 d2 -- flag ) Compare
; compares two d values (signed)

COLON 2,"D>"
DGRE:
ld  temp0, Y+
ld  temp1, Y+
ld  temp2, Y+
ld  temp3, Y+
ld  temp4, Y+
ld  temp5, Y+
cp  temp4, temp0
cpc temp5, temp1
cpc temp2, tosl
cpc temp3, tosh
DGRE1:
movw tosl,zerol
brlt DGRE2
brbs 1, DGRE2
sbiw tosl,1
ret
DGRE2:
ret

; D+ ( d1 d2 -- d3) Arithmetics
; add double cell values

COLON 2,"D+"
DPLUS:
```

```
ld  temp2, Y+
ld  temp3, Y+
ld  temp4, Y+
ld  temp5, Y+
ld  temp6, Y+
ld  temp7, Y+
add  temp2, temp6
adc  temp3, temp7
adc  tosl, temp4
adc  tosh, temp5
st  -Y, temp3
st  -Y, temp2
ret

; D- ( d1 d2 -- d3 ) Arithmetics
; subtract double cell values

COLON 2,"D-"
DMINUS:
ld  temp2, Y+
ld  temp3, Y+
ld  temp4, Y+

ld  temp5, Y+
ld  temp6, Y+
ld  temp7, Y+
sub  temp6, temp2
sbc  temp7, temp3
sbc  temp4, tosl
sbc  temp5, tosh
st  -Y, temp7
st  -Y, temp6
movw  tosl,  temp4
ret
```

1+	Increment the top item on the parameter stack by 1.
1-	Decrement the top item on the parameter stack by 1.
2+	Increment the top item on the parameter stack by 2.
2-	Decrement the top item on the parameter stack by 2.

>	Compare the top two items of the parameter stack. Return a true flag if the second item is greater than the top item. Stack items are assumed to be signed integers
D>	Compare the top four items of the parameter stack as two signed double integers. Return a true flag if the second double integer is greater than the top doble integer. Stack items are assumed to be signed double integers
D+	Add the top four items of the parameter stack as two signed double integers. Return a signed double integer sum.
D-	Subtract the top four items of the parameter stack as two signed double integers. Subtract top double integer from the second double integer, and return the difference as a signed double integer.

```
; ALLOT ( n -- )
; Allocate n bytes to the code dictionary.

 COLON 5,"ALLOT"
ALLOT:
 CALL DPP
 JMP  PSTOR

;  IALLOT ( n -- )
; Allocate n bytes to the code dictionary.

 COLON 6,"IALLOT"
IALLOT:
 CALL CPP
 JMP  PSTOR

;  , ( w -- )
; Compile an integer into the
; code dictionary.
COLON 1,","
COMMA:
 CALL CPP
 CALL AT
 CALL DUPP
 CALL CELLP ;cell boundary
```

```
 CALL CPP
 CALL STORE
 JMP  ISTOR

;   call, ( ca -- )
; Assemble a call instruction to ca.

; COLON 5,"call,"
CALLC:
 CALL DOLIT
 .DW  CALLL
 CALL COMMA
 RJMP COMMA ;328 long call

;   [COMPILE] ( -- ; <string> )
; Compile the next immediate word into
;  code dictionary.

 COLON IMEDD+9,"[COMPILE]"
BCOMP:
 CALL TICK
 RJMP CALLC

;   COMPILE ( -- )
; Compile the next address in colon list
; to code dictionary.

 COLON COMPO+7,"COMPILE" COMPI:
 CALL RFROM
 CALL DUPP
 CALL AT
 CALL COMMA  ;compile call instruction
 CALL CELLP
 CALL DUPP
 CALL AT
 CALL COMMA  ;compile address
 CALL CELLP
 CALL TOR
 RET         ;adjust return address

;   LITERAL ( w -- )
; Compile tos to code dictionary
; as an integer literal.
```

```
COLON 7,"LITERAL" LITER:
CALL DOLIT
.DW  DOLIT
CALL CALLC
RJMP COMMA

;  $," ( -- )
; Compile a literal string up to next " .

; COLON 3,'$'
; .DB  ',',''''
STRCQ:
 CALL DOLIT
 .DW  ''''
 CALL WORDD ;move string to
          ; code dictionary
 CALL DUPP
 CALL CAT
 CALL TWOSL
 CALL TOR
STRCQ1:
 CALL DUPP
 CALL AT
 CALL COMMA
 CALL CELLP
 CALL DONXT
 .DW  STRCQ1
 JMP  DROP
```

ALLOT	Allocats n bytes of RAM memory on bottom of the free RAM space. System variable DP points to the bottom of free RAM space.
IALLOT	Allocate n bytes of flash memory on the top of the dictionary. System variable CP points to the top of the dictionary.
,	It is the most primitive compiler command. It compiles an integer w to dictionary in the flash memory, and add the new item to the growing command list of the current command under

	construction. This is the primitive compiler upon which the FORTH compiler rests.
CALL,	Compile or assemble a subroutine call instruction with the code field address on the parameter stack as destination. Compound commands are compiled as lists of subroutine calls.
[COMPILE]	Compile the code field address of the next command in the input stream. It is used to compile commands, which would otherwise be executed while compiling.
COMPILE	Compile the code field address of the next command in the input stream. It forces compilation of a command at run time.
LITERAL	Compile an integer literal. It first compiles a call doLIT machine instruction, followed by an integer value from the parameter stack. When doLIT is executed, it extracts the integer in the next program word and pushes it on the parameter stack.
$,"	Compile a string literal. String text is taken from the input stream and terminated by a double quote. A token (such as ." | or $" |) must be compiled before the string to form a sting literal.
?UNIQUE	Display a warning message to show that the name of a new command is the same as a command already in the dictionary.
$,n	Build a new header in the dictionary using the name string already packed in the WORD buffer. Fill in the link field with the address in LAST. The top of the dictionary is now the code field of a new command, ready to accept commands and tokens.
$COMPILE	Process a string at a, and compile a new token, a call instruction, in the dictionary. This dictionary pointer in CP is incremented, and is ready to compile the next token.

OVERT	Link a new command to the dictionary and make it available for a dictionary search. OVERT changes CONTEXT to point to the name field of this new command, and extends the dictionary chain to include a new command.
;	Terminate a compound command. Compile a ret instruction to terminate a token list. Link this command to the dictionary, and change the text interpreter to interpreting mode.
]	Activate compiling mode by writing the address of $COMPILE into system variable 'EVAL.
:	Create a new compound command. Take the next input string to build a new header. Now, its code field is on top of the command dictionary, and is ready to accept new tokens.

5.5.5 Structure Commands

Immediate commands are not compiled as tokens by the compiler. Instead, they are executed by the compiler immediately. They are used to build control structures in compound commands. Immediate commands has its IMMEDIATE lexicon bit set, in the length byte of the name field. The control structures used in 328eForth are the following:

Conditional branch	IF ... THEN
	IF ... ELSE ... THEN
Finite loop	FOR ... NEXT
	FOR ... AFT ... THEN... NEXT
Infinite loop	BEGIN ... AGAIN
Indefinite loop	BEGIN ... UNTIL
	BEGIN ... WHILE ... REPEAT

A control structure contains one or more address literals with ?branch, branch and next commands, which causes execution to branch out of the normal sequence. The control structure commands are immediate commands which compile the address literals and resolve the branch address.

One should note that BEGIN and THEN do not compile any token. They set up or resolve control structures in compound commands. IF, ELSE, WHILE, UNTIL, and AGAIN do compile address literals with branching tokens.

I use two characters a and A to denote some addresses on the data stack. a points to a location to where a branch commands would jump to. A points to a location where a new address will be stored when the address is resolved.

```
;; Structures

;  BEGIN ( -- a )
; Start an infinite or
; indefinite loop structure.

 COLON IMEDD+5,"BEGIN"
BEGIN:
 CALL CPP
 JMP  AT

;  FOR ( -- a )
; Start a FOR-NEXT loop structure in a
; colon definition.
```

```
 COLON IMEDD+3,"FOR" FOR:
 CALL DOLIT  .DW  TOR
 CALL CALLC
 RJMP BEGIN

;  NEXT ( a -- )
; Terminate a FOR-NEXT loop structure.

 COLON IMEDD+4,"NEXT" NEXT:
 CALL DOLIT
 .DW  DONXT
 CALL CALLC
 CALL TWOSL
 RJMP COMMA
```

```
    ;  UNTIL ( a -- )
    ; Terminate a BEGIN-UNTIL indefinite
    ; loop structure.

    COLON IMEDD+5,"UNTIL"
UNTIL:
        CALL DOLIT
        .DW  QBRAN
        CALL CALLC
        CALL TWOSL
        RJMP COMMA

    ;  AGAIN ( a -- )
    ; Terminate a BEGIN-AGAIN infinite
    ; loop structure.

    COLON IMEDD+5,"AGAIN"
 AGAIN:
        CALL DOLIT
        .DW  BRAN
        CALL CALLC
        CALL TWOSL
        RJMP COMMA
```

BEGIN	Start a loop structure. It pushes an address a on the parameter stack. a points to the top of the dictionary where new tokens will be compiled. If begins an infinite loop or an indefinite loop.
FOR	Compile a >R token and pushes the address of the next token a on the parameter stack. It starts a FOR-NEXT loop.
NEXT	Compile a next token with a target address a on the top of the parameter stack. It resolves a FOR NEXT loop.
UNTIL	Compile a ?branch token with a target address a on the top of the parameter stack. It resolves a BEGIN-UNTIL loop.

AGAIN	Compile a branch token with a target address a on the top of the parameter stack. It resolves a BEGIN-AGAIN loop.

```
; IF ( -- A )
; Begin a conditional branch structure.

COLON IMEDD+2,"IF" IFF:
CALL DOLIT
.DW QBRAN
CALL CALLC
CALL BEGIN
CALL DOLIT
.DW 2
RJMP IALLOT

; AHEAD ( -- A )
; Compile a forward branch instruction.

; COLON IMEDD+5,"AHEAD" AHEAD:
CALL DOLIT
.DW BRAN
CALL CALLC
CALL BEGIN
CALL DOLIT
.DW 2
JMP IALLOT

; REPEAT ( A a -- )
; Terminate a BEGIN-WHILE-REPEAT
; indefinite loop.

COLON IMEDD+6,"REPEAT" REPEA:
CALL AGAIN
CALL BEGIN
CALL TWOSL
CALL SWAPP
JMP ISTOR

; THEN ( A -- )
; Terminate a conditional branch structure.
```

```
COLON IMEDD+4,"THEN" THENN:
CALL BEGIN
CALL TWOSL
CALL SWAPP
JMP  ISTOR

;  AFT ( a -- a1 A )
; Jump to THEN in a FOR-AFT-THEN-NEXT loop
; the first time through.

COLON IMEDD+3,"AFT" AFT:
CALL DROP
CALL AHEAD
CALL BEGIN
JMP  SWAPP

;  ELSE ( A -- A )
; Start the false clause in an
; IF-ELSE-THEN structure.

COLON IMEDD+4,"ELSE" ELSEE:
CALL AHEAD
CALL SWAPP
JMP  THENN

;  WHILE ( a -- A a )
; Conditional branch out of a
; BEGIN-WHILE-REPEAT loop.

COLON IMEDD+5,"WHILE"
WHILE:
CALL IFF
JMP  SWAPP
```

IF	Compile a ?branch address literal and pushes its address, a, is left on the parameter stack. It starts a IF-ELSE-THEN or a IF-THEN branch structure.
AHEAD	Compile a branch address literal and pushes its address, a, is left on the parameter stack. It starts a AHEAD-THEN branch structure.
REPEAT	Compile a branch token with a target address a on the top of the parameter stack. It resolves a BEGIN-WHILE-REPEAT loop.
THEN	Resolve the address in a branch token whose address is a on the top of the parameter stack. It resolves a IF-ELSE-TEHN or IF-THEN branch structure.
AFT	Compile a branch literal and leaves its address as A, It also replaces the address a left by FOR with the address a1 of the next token. A will be used by THEN to resolve the AFT-THEN branch structure, and a1 will be used by NEXT to resolve the loop structure.
ELSE	Compile a branch token, and use the address of the next token to resolve the address field of ?branch token in a, as left by IF. It also replaces a with A, the address of its address field for THEN to resolve. ELSE starts the false clause in the IF-ELSE-THEN branch structure.
WHILE	Compile a ?branch token and leave its address, A, on the stack. Address a left by BEGIN is swapped to the top of the parameter stack. WHILE is used to start the true clause in the BEGIN-WHILE-REPEAT loop.

```
;  ABORT" ( -- ; <string> )
; Conditional abort with an error message.

 COLON IMEDD+6,"ABORT"
 .DB  '"'
ABRTQ:
 CALL DOLIT
 .DW  ABORQ
 CALL CALLC
```

```
CALL STRCQ RET

; $" ( -- ; <string> )
; Compile an inline string literal.

COLON IMEDD+2,'$'
.DB '"'
STRQ:
CALL DOLIT
.DW STRQP
CALL CALLC
CALL STRCQ
RET

; ." ( -- ; <string> )
; Compile an inline string literal to be
; typed out at run time.

COLON IMEDD+2,'.'
.DB '"'
DOTQ:
CALL DOLIT
.DW DOTQP
CALL CALLC
CALL STRCQ
RET
```

ABORT"	Compile an error message as a string literal. This error message is display at run time if the top item on the parameter stack is true, and the rest of the tokens in this compound command are skipped and eForth enters the interpreter loop in QUIT. This is the programmed response to an error condition.
."	Compile a string literal which will be printed when it is executed in run time. This is the best way to present messages to you in an application.

$"	Compile a string literal. When it is executed, only the address of the string is pushed on the parameter stack. Later commands can use this address to access the string and individual characters in the string as a string array.

5.5.6 Name Compiler

We had seen how tokens and structures are compiled into the code field of a compound command in the dictionary. To build a new command, we have to build its header first. A header consists of a link field and a name field. Here are the commands to build the header.

```
;; Name compiler

;   ?UNIQUE ( a -- a )
; Display a warning message if the word
; already exists.

; COLON 7,"?UNIQUE" UNIQU:
```

```
 CALL DUPP
 CALL NAMEQ ;?name exists
 CALL QBRAN
 .DW  UNIQ1
 CALL DOTQP ;redefinitions are OK
 .DB  7," reDef " ; but the user should  be warned
 CALL OVER
 CALL COUNT
 CALL TYPES ;just in case its not planned
UNIQ1:
 JMP  DROP

;   $,n ( na -- )
; Build a new dictionary name using
; the string at na.

; COLON 3,"$,n" SNAME:
 CALL DUPP
 CALL CAT ;?null input
 CALL QBRAN
 .DW  SNAM2
 CALL UNIQU ;?redefinition
 CALL LAST
 CALL AT
 CALL COMMA ;compile link
 CALL CPP
 CALL AT
 CALL LAST
 CALL STORE ;save new nfa in LAST
 CALL DUPP
 CALL CAT
 CALL TWOSL ;na count/2
 CALL TOR
SNAME1:
 CALL DUPP
 CALL AT
 CALL COMMA ;compile name
 CALL CELLP
 CALL  DONXT
 .DW  SNAME1
 JMP  DROP
SNAM2:
 CALL STRQP
 .DB  5," name" ;null input
 JMP  ERROR
```

?UNIQUE	Display a warning message to show that the name of a new command already exists in the dictionary. FORTH does not prevent your reusing the same name for different commands. However, giving the same name to many different commands often causes problems in software projects. It is to be avoided if possible and ?UNIQUE reminds you of it.
$,n	Build a new header with a name string at RAM address na. It first build a link field with an address pointing to the name field of the prior command, and then copies the string at na to build a name field. The top of dictionary is the code field of the new command, and tokens can be compiled.

5.5.7 FORTH Compiler

```
;; FORTH compiler

;  $COMPILE ( a -- )
; Compile next word to code dictionary
; as a token or literal.

; COLON 8,"$COMPILE" SCOMP:
 CALL NAMEQ
 CALL QDUP  ;?defined
 CALL QBRAN
 .DW  SCOM2  CALL IAT
 CALL DOLIT
 .DW  IMEDD
 CALL ANDD  ;?immediate
 CALL QBRAN
 .DW  SCOM1
 JMP  EXECU
SCOM1:
 CALL TWOSL
 JMP  CALLC
SCOM2:
 CALL NUMBQ
 CALL QBRAN
```

```
 .DW  SCOM3
 JMP  LITER
SCOM3:
 JMP  ERROR ;error

;  OVERT ( -- )
; Link a new word into the
; current vocabulary.

; COLON 5,"OVERT" OVERT:
 CALL LAST
 CALL AT
 CALL CNTXT
 JMP  STORE

;  ;( -- )
; Terminate a colon definition.

 COLON IMEDD+COMPO+1,";" SEMIS:
 CALL DOLIT
 .DW  RETT
 CALL COMMA
 CALL LBRAC
 JMP  OVERT
```

$COMPILE	Build the token list of a new compound command in its code field, which is on the top of the dictionary. It takes a string address a on the top of the parameter stack, search dictionary for a matching command, and adds a token to the token list. If the string is not a valid command, it is converted to a number, and a integer literal added to the token list. If the string is not a number, abort the compilation process and return to the text interpreter loop in QUIT. If the string is the name of an immediate command, this command is not compiled, but executed immediately. Immediate commands are tools used by the compiler to build structures in compound commands.

OVERT	Link a new command to the dictionary and thus makes it available for dictionary searches. When a new header is build, its name field address is stored in system variable LAST, and it is not yet linked to the dictionary which starts at CONTEXT. OVERT copies the name field address in LAST to CONTEXT and links the new command to the dictionary. It is used to protect the dictionary so that new commands not compiled successfully will not be compiled incorrectly into later compound commands.
;	Terminate a new compound command. It compiles an ret machine instruction to terminate the new token list, links this new command to the dictionary, and then returns to the text interpreter by storing the code field address of $INTERPRET into system variable 'EVAL.

```
;  ]( -- )
; Start compiling the words in the
; input stream.

 COLON 1,"]"
RBRAC:
 CALL DOLIT
 .DW  SCOMP*2
 CALL TEVAL
 JMP  STORE

;  : ( -- ; <string> )
; Start a new colon definition
; using next word as its name.

 COLON 1,":"
COLONN:
 CALL TOKEN
 CALL SNAME
 JMP  RBRAC

;  IMMEDIATE ( -- )
```

```
; Make the last compiled word
; an immediate word.

 COLON 9,"IMMEDIATE" IMMED:
 CALL DOLIT
 .DW  IMEDD
 CALL LAST
 CALL AT
 CALL IAT
 CALL ORR
 CALL LAST
 CALL AT
JMP  ISTOR
```

]	Turn the text interpreter to a compiler by storing the code field address of $COMPILE into system variable 'EVAL..
:	Create a new header and start a new compound command. It takes the following string in the input stream to be the name of the new command. The dictionary is ready to accept a token list.] turns the text interpreter into compiler, which will compile the following text strings to build a new compound command. The new compound command is terminated by ;.
IMMEDIATE	Set the immediate lexicon bit in the name field of the new command. When the compiler encounters a command with this bit set, it will not compile this words into the token list under construction, but execute it immediately. This bit allows structure commands to build special structures in compound commands, and to deal with special conditions when the compiler is running.

5.5.8 Defining Commands

Defining commands are molds which can be used to create classes of commands which share the same run time execution behavior. In 328eForth, we have these defining commands: : , CREATE, CONSTANT and VARIABLE.

```
;; Defining words

;   CREATE ( -- ; <string> )
; Compile a new array entry without
; allocating code space.

 COLON 6,"CREATE"
CREAT:
 CALL TOKEN
 CALL SNAME
 CALL OVERT
  CALL DOLIT
 .DW  DOVAR
 CALL CALLC
 CALL DPP
 CALL AT
 JMP  COMMA

;   CONSTANT ( n -- ; <string> )
; Compile a constant.

 COLON 8,"CONSTANT" CONST:
 CALL TOKEN
 CALL SNAME
 CALL OVERT
 CALL DOLIT
 .DW  DOVAR
 CALL CALLC
 JMP  COMMA

;   VARIABLE ( -- ; <string> )
; Compile a new variable uninitialized.

 COLON 8,"VARIABLE" VARIA:
 CALL CREAT
```

```
CALL DOLIT
.DW  2
JMP  ALLOT

;=============================================
.EQU LASTN = _LINK*2 ;l ast name address in
                ; name dictionary
.EQU DTOP = $140 ; next available memory in
             ; name dictionary
.EQU CTOP = pc*2 ; next available memory in
             ; code dictionary


;=============================================
```

CREATE	Create a new data array in RAM memory without allocating memory. When commands created by CREATE is executed, they will push their respective RAM addresses on the parameter stack. Memory space of an actual array is allocated using ALLOT command.
VARIABE	Create a new command with a doVAR token followed by a pointer to RAM memory and allocate 2 bytes of space in RAM memory. When a variable commands is executed, it pushes the RAM address on the parameter stack.
CONSTANT	Create a new command with a doVAR token followed by the constant value. When a constant command is executed, it pushes the constant value on the parameter stack.

6. Conclusions

What I give you in 328eForth is that in 5156 bytes, you have a programming language, an interactive operating system, and all the debugging tools to develop applications on Arduino Uno, for Arduino Uno. The complete source code of 328eForth.asm is only 54 Kbytes long, comparing to 232 MB hogged by Arduino 0022. It is an organic system, which can grow to accommodate any application that ATmega328P microcontroller can host. It allows you to read all its CPU and I/O registers, and all its data and program memories. It also allows you to change the I/O registers and memories, and to add new commands to the flash memory. By adding new commands, you can extend the 328eForth system and build a new system which will do what you want it to do.

In 328eForth, I try to reduce the FORTH language to its bare minimum, so that you can learn this programming language quickly, and to use it to do useful work. ATmega328P, like all the newer microcontrollers available now, contains many powerful and complicated I/O devices, and it takes the AVR Data Book 566 pages to explain them. With 328eForth, you can examine all the I/O registers and modify them to make the I/O devices work the way you want them to work. There is no better way to study the AVR Data Book than to read the book along with 328eForth, modifying the I/O registers and observe what the I/O devices do. 328eForth is a worthy companion to the AVR Data Book.

Arduino Uno is an excellent platform for FORTH. FORTH allows you to develop substantial applications quickly and produce high quality code. You write commands in small modules which can be tested exhaustively. Fully tested commands can be used to build more powerful commands at higher conceptual levels, until the last command, which becomes the application. This last command can be used to configure a turnkey system, so that it will be executed when the system boots up. You can do all these things with 328eForth on Auduino Uno.

FORTH is a programming paradigm very different from conventional programming languages and operating systems. It can be embedded into a small microcontroller, and empowers you to make the best use of the limited resources available in a microcontroller. I hope you will learn this paradigm and enjoy these benefits:

Integrated operating system and programming language on a small chip
Interactive command interpreter
Incremental compilation of new commands

Bottom up coding and debugging
Naturally structured programming
Ready access to memory and I/O registers
Ease in building turnkey applications

In explaining how this system is constructed, every step in the way, I hope to lay to rest these myths, that computers are complicate, programming languages are complicated, and operating systems are complicated. All these things can be very simple, and can be understood by ordinary people and ordinary engineers. If you understand this 328eForth system completely, the understanding can be carried over to any computer and microcontrollers.

People using computers are trained to be slaves. You are taught to push certain buttons, and your are taught to push certain keys. Then, you get employed to push buttons and keys to work as slaves. Computers, programming languages, and operating systems are made complicated to enslave people.

Computers are not complicated beyond comprehension. Programming languages and operating systems do not have to be complicated. If you get a sharp knife, you can be the master of your destination. 328eForth is a sharp knife. Go use it.

7 328eForth Commands

Stack Comments:

Stack inputs and outputs are shown in the form:

(input1 input2 ... -- output1 output2 ...)

Stack Abbreviations of Number Types

flag	Boolean flag, either 0 or -1
char	ASCII character or a byte
n	16 bit number
addr	16 bit address
d	32 bit number

Stack Manipulation Commands

?DUP	(n -- n n | 0)	Duplicate top of stack if it is not 0.
DUP	(n1 -- n2)	Duplicate top of stack.
DROP	(n --)	Discard top of stack.
SWAP	(n1 n2 -- n2 n1)	Exchange top two stack items.
OVER	(n1 n2 -- n1 n2 n1)	Make copy of second item on stack.
ROT	(n1 n2 n3 -- n2 n3 n1)	Rotate third item to top.
PICK	(n -- n1)	Zero based, duplicate nth item to top. (e.g. 0 PICK is DUP).
>R	(n --)	Move top item to return stack for temporary storage.
R>	(-- n)	Retrieve top item from return stack.
R@	(-- n)	Copy top of return stack onto stack.
2DUP	(d -- d d)	Duplicate double number on top of stack.
2DROP	(d1 d2 --)	Discard two double numbers on top of stack
DEPTH	(-- n)	Count number of items on stack.

Arithmetic Commands

+	(n1 n2 -- n3)	Add n1 and n2.
-	(n1 n2 -- n3)	Subtract n2 from n1 (n1-n2=n3).
*	(n1 n2 -- n3)	Multiply. n3=n1*n2
/	(n1 n2 -- n3)	Division, signed (n3= n1/n2).
1+	(n -- n+1)	Increment n.
1-	(n -- n-1)	Decrement n.
2+	(n -- n+2)	Add two to n.
2-	(n -- n-2)	Subtract two from n.
2*	(n -- n*2)	Logic left shift.
2/	(n -- n/2)	Logic right shift.
UM+	(n1 n2 -- nd)	Unsigned addition, double precision result.
UM*	(n1 n2 -- nd)	Unsigned multiply, double precision result.
M*	(n n -- d)	Signed multiply. Return double product.
UM/MOD	(nd n1 -- mod quot)	Unsigned division with double precision dividend.
M/MOD	(d n -- mod quot)	Signed floored divide of double by single. Return mod and quotient.
MOD	(n1 n2 -- mod)	Modulus, signed (remainder of n1/n2).
/MOD	(n1 n2 -- mod quot)	Division with both remainder and quotient.
*/MOD	(n1 n2 n3 -- n4 n5)	Multiply and then divide (n1*n2/n3)
*/	(n1 n2 n3 -- n4)	Like */MOD, but with quotient only.
ABS	(n1 -- n2)	If n1 is negative, n2 is its two's complement.
NEGATE	(n1 -- n2)	Two's complement.
MAX	(n1 n2 -- n3)	n3 is the larger of n1 and n2.
MIN	(n1 n2 -- n3)	n3 is the smaller of n1 and n2.
WITHIN	(n1 n2 n3 -- flag)	Return true if n1 is within range of n2 and n3. (n2 <= n1 < n3)
DNEGATE	(d1 -- d2)	Negate double number. Two's complement.
D+	(d1 d2 -- d3)	Add double numbers.
D-	(d1 d2 -- d3)	Subtract double numbers.

Logic and Comparison Commands

AND	(n1 n2 -- n3)	Logical bit-wise AND.
OR	(n1 n2 -- n3)	Logical bit-wise OR.
XOR	(n1 n2 -- n3)	Logical bit-wise exclusive OR.
INVERT	(n1 -- n2)	Bit-wise one's complement.
0<	(n -- flag)	True if n is negative.
U<	(n1 n2 -- flag)	True if n1 less than n2. Unsigned compare.
<	(n1 n2 -- flag)	True if n1 less than n2.
=	(n1 n2 -- flag)	True if n1 equals n2.
>	(n1 n2 -- flag)	True if n1 greater than n2.
D>	(d1 d2 -- flag)	True if d1 greater than d2.

RAM Memory Commands

@	(addr -- n)	Replace addr by number at addr.
C@	(addr -- char)	Fetch least-significant byte only.
!	(n addr --)	Store n at addr.
C!	(char addr --)	Store least-significant byte only.
+!	(n addr --)	Add n to number at addr.
COUNT	(addr1 -- addr+1 char)	Move string count from memory onto stack.
ALLOT	(n --)	Add n bytes to the RAM pointer DP.
HERE	(-- addr)	Address of next available RAM memory location.
PAD	(-- addr)	Address of a scratch area of at least 64 bytes.
TIB	(-- addr)	Address of terminal input buffer.
CMOVE	(addr1 addr2 n --)	Move n bytes starting at memory addr1 to addr2.
FILL	(addr n char --)	Fill n bytes of memory at addr with char.

Flash Memory Commands

I@	(addr -- n)	Replace addr by number at flash memory addr.
IC@	(addr -- char)	Fetch a byte from flash memory addr.
I!	(n addr --)	Store n at flash memory addr.
ICOUNT	(addr1 -- addr+1 char)	Move string count from flash memory onto stack.
IALLOT	(n --)	Add n bytes to the flash memory pointer CP.
ITYPE	(addr n --)	Display a string of n characters in flash starting at address addr.
READ	(addr1 addr2 --)	Read 128 bytes from flash memory addr1 to RAM memory addr2.
WRITE	(addr1 addr2 --)	Write 128 bytes from RAM memory addr1 to flash memory addr2.
ERASE	(addr --)	Erase an 128 byte page in flash memory at addr.
FLUSH	(--)	Write modified flash buffers back to flash memory.

System Variables

'BOOT	(-- addr)	Contain address of application command to boot.
BASE	(-- addr)	Contain radix for number conversion
TMP	(-- addr)	Temporary scratch pad
SPAN	(-- addr)	Contain actual number of characters received by EXPECT
>IN	(-- addr)	Contain character offset into the input stream buffer.
#TIB	(-- addr)	Contain current length of terminal input buffer (TIB).
'TIB	(-- addr)	Contain current address of terminal input buffer (TIB)
'EVAL	(-- addr)	Contain interpreter or compiler to evaluate a command.
HLD	(-- addr)	Contain pointer to numeric string under construction.
CONTEXT	(-- addr)	Contain name field address of last command in dictionary
CP	(-- addr)	Contain first free address in flash memory
DP	(-- addr)	Contain first free address in RAM memory
LAST	(-- addr)	Contain name field address of command under compilation

Terminal Input-Output Commands

EMIT	(char --)	Display char.
KEY	(-- char)	Get an ASCII character from the keyboard.
?KEY	(-- char -1 | 0)	Return an ASCII character from the keyboard and a true flag. Return false flag if no character available.
.	(n --)	Display number n with a trailing blank.
U.	(n --)	Display an unsigned integer with a trailing blank.
.R	(n1 n2 --)	Display signed number n1 right justified in n2 character field.
U.R	(n1 n2 --)	Display unsigned number n1 right justified in n2 character field.
?	(addr --)	Display contents at memory addr.
<#	(--)	Start numeric output string conversion.
#	(n1 -- n2)	Convert next digit of number and add to output string
#S	(n --)	Convert all significant digits in n to output string.
HOLD	(char --)	Add char to output string.
SIGN	(n --)	If n is negative, add a minus sign to the output string.
#>	(xd -- addr n)	Terminate numeric string, leaving addr and count for TYPE.
CR	(--)	Display a new line.
SPACE	(--)	Display a space.
SPACES	(n --)	Display n spaces.
EXPECT	(addr n --)	Accept n characters into buffer at addr.
CHAR	(-- char)	Parse next command and return its first character.
TYPE	(addr n --)	Display a string of n characters starting at address addr.
BL	(-- 32)	Return ASCII Blank character.
DECIMAL	(--)	Set number base to decimal.
HEX	(--)	Set number base to hexadecimal.

Compiler and Interpreter Commands

:<name>	(--)	Begin a colon definition of <name>.
;	(--)	Terminate execution of a colon definition.
CREATE <name>	(--)	Dictionary entry with no parameter field space reserved.
VARIABL E <name>	(--)	Defines a variable. At run-time, <name> leaves its address.
CONSTAN T <name>	(n --)	Defines a constant. At run-time, n is left on the stack.
,	(n --)	Compile n to the dictionary in flash memory
IMMEDIA TE	(--)	Cause last-defined command to execute even within a colon definition.
COMPILE <name>	(--)	<name> is compiled to dictionary.
[COMPILE] <name>	(--)	Immediate command <name> is compiled to dictionary.
LITERAL	(n --)	Compile literal number n. At run-time, n is pushed on the stack.
[	(--)	Switch from compilation to interpretation.
]	(--)	Switch from interpretation to compilation.
WORD<tex t>	(char -- addr)	Get the char delimited string <text> from the input stream and leave as a counted string at addr.
(comment)	(--)	Ignore comment text.
\ comment	(--)	Ignore comment till end of line.
." <text>"	(--)	Compile <text> message. At run-time display text message.
.(<text>)	(--)	Display <text> from the input stream.
$" <text>"	(-- addr)	Compile <text> message. At run-time return its address.
ABORT" <text>"	(flag --)	Compile <test> message. At run-time display message and abort if flag is true. Otherwise, ignore message and continue.
COLD	(--)	Start eForth system.
QUIT	(--)	Return to interpret mode, clear data and return stacks.
QUERY	(--)	Accept input stream to terminal input buffer.
NAME>	(addr1 -- addr2)	Traverse name field at addr1 and return code field address

		addr2.
NUMBER?	(addr -- n -1 | addr 0)	Convert a number string to integer. Push a flag on tos.
EXECUTE	(addr --)	Execute command definition at addr.
@EXECUTE	(addr --)	Execute command definition whose execution address is in addr.
EXIT	(--)	Terminate execution of a colon definition.

Compiler Structure Commands

IF	(flag --)	If flag is zero, branches forward to ELSE or THEN.
ELSE	(--)	Branch forward to THEN.
THEN	(--)	Terminate a IF-ELSE-THEN structure.
FOR	(n --)	Setup loop with n as index. Repeat loop n+1 times.
NEXT	(--)	Decrement loop index by 1 and branch back to FOR. Terminate FOR-NEXT loop when index is negative.
AFT	(--)	Branch forward to THEN in a loop to skip the first round
BEGIN	(--)	Start an indefinite loop.
AGAIN	(--)	Branch backward to BEGIN.
UNTIL	(flag --)	Branch backward to BEGIN if flag is false. If flag is true, terminate BEGIN-UNTIL loop.
WHILE	(flag --)	If flag is false, branch forward to terminate BEGIN-WHILE-REPEAT loop. If flag is true, continue execution till REPEAT.
REPEAT	(--)	Resolve WHILE clause. Branch backward to BEGIN.

Utility Commands

' <name>	(-- addr)	Look up <name> in the dictionary. Return execution address.
WORDS	(--)	Display all eForth commands
DUMP	(addr --)	Dump 128 bytes of RAM memory starting from addr.
IDUMP	(addr --)	Dump 128 bytes of flash memory starting from addr.
.S	(--)	Dump the parameter stack.

8 Some Examples

```
\ Hello, World                                  WFR 2011-01-27
\ Modified for 328eForth, 23mar11cht

\ must have marker.txt installed

marker chop-hello

: hello cr ." Hello World!" ;

: test ." Testing " 1 . 2 . 3 . ."  Anyone out there?" ;

flush

hello

test

chop-hello
```

```
\ Port Input Output for AmForth                WFR 2011-01-27
\ loaded as  io-core.txt
\ Modified for 328eForth, 23mar11cht

\ manually begin with chop-io entered

chop-io
marker chop-io  \ a forget point

: mask ( bit# --- port_mask  convert bit to 8 bit mask)
     1 swap lshift  ;

: DDR  \ port --- port' adjust input port# to DDR
    1+ ;

: Output \ port --- port adjust input port# to output
    2 + ;

: RegFrom \ Reg mask --- value  read masked bits from register
        \ To read all bits:  PortB true RegFrom -> value
     swap c@  and ;

: RegTo \ Reg mask new ---  write masked new into register
     over and >r   invert over c@ and   r> or  swap c! ;

: PoBiI/O  \ port bit direction --- configure bit in/out
    rot DDR   rot mask   rot RegTo ;

: PoBiOut  \ port bit --- configure as output
    true  PoBiI/O ;

: PoBiRead  \ port bit --- value  read bit value from port
     mask RegFrom ;

: PoBiHi  \ port bit --- set port bit 0..7 high
     swap Output swap mask true  RegTo ;

: PoBiLo   \ port bit --- clear port bit 0..7 low
     swap Output swap mask false RegTo ;
```

```
: PoBiIn   \ port bit --- configure as input,  no pull-up
    2dup false PoBiI/O   PoBiLo ( pullup inactive) ;

: PoBiInPu \ port bit --- configure as input with pull-up
    2dup false PoBiI/O   PoBiHi ( pullup active) ;

\ read bits from register  Reg#         select      RegFrom
\ write bits to register   Reg#         select bits RegTo
\ write 1-bit to register  Reg#    5 mask true      RegTo
\ write 0-bit to register  Reg#    5 mask false     RegTo
\ configure bits as output PortB DDR    select True RegTo
\ write bits to output     PortB Output select bits RegTo
\ configure bit as output  PortB     LED            PoBiOut
\ bit as input with pullup PortB     Switch3        PoBiInPu
\ read bit from port       PortB     Switch3        PoBiRead
\ write 1-bit to port      PortB     LED            PoBiHi
\ write 0-bit to port      PortB     LED            PoBiLo
\ Note, when initializing a 16 bit register, TCNT1 etc. it
\  must be written directly hi/lo not using RegTo.
\  The proper form to clear is:    TCNT1hi false c!
\                         then:    TCNT1lo false c!
\

\ end of io-core.txt
flush
```

```
\ KEYER.txt   input of iambic key              WFR 2011-01-27
\ Modified for 328eForth, 23mar11cht

\ must have io-core.txt and tone.txt installed

chop-keyer

decimal

marker chop-keyer  ( a forget point)

$23 value PortB   0 value dah-in  1 value dit-in

: setup-key   \  ---  set inputs with pullups
   PortB  dah-in PoBiInPu
   PortB  dit-in PoBiInPu    ;

1 value Last-in  \ dit or dah last sent

: last?  \ n -- n   convert both into last sent inverted
  dup 3 = if drop Last-in  3 xor then
  dup to Last-in ( save for next time)  ;

: sense-key ( ---  bits true | false
   PortB 3 RegFrom  3 xor \  read & invert two low bits
   dup  if last? true else drop false then ;

10 value WPM  \ words per minute

: element-delay  1200 * WPM / ms ;

: dit tone-on 1 element-delay tone-off 1 element-delay ;

: dah tone-on 3 element-delay tone-off 1 element-delay ;

: next-character 2 element-delay ;  \ 3 total

: next-word      6 element-delay ;  \ 7 total
```

```
: V   dit dit dit dah next-character ;

: demo  \ iambic keyer
    setup-key
    begin
      sense-key
        if  1 and if dah else dit then then
    ?key until ;

: sos   dit dit dit next-character dah dah dah next-character
        dit dit dit next-word ;

flush
```

```
\  Marker.txt                                    WFR 2010-10-22
\ Defines a word which resets the dictionary when executed.
\  Due  to  three  memory  spaces  the  traditional  FORGET  is
impractial.
\ Modified for 328eForth, 23mar11cht

\ Extend eForth first, 22mar11cht
: DOES R> LAST @ NAME> 2+ I! ;
\ specific for subroutine thread code.  see VALUE and MARKER.

: VALUE ( n --, interpret ) VARIABLE DP @ 2- ! DOES R> 2* I@ @ ;
\ compile a pointer in flash, access data in RAM

: [TO] ( n --, interpret ) ' 4 + I@ ! ;
\ change value while interpreting

: to ( n --, compile ) R> DUP   1+ 2* I@   2+ 2* I@   SWAP 2+ >R
! ;
\ compiled in colon word to change value at run time

: TRUE ( -- -1 ) FFFF ;
: FALSE ( -- 0 ) 0 ;
: LSHIFT ( n --, logic left shift ) FOR AFT 2* THEN NEXT ;
: RSHIFT ( n --, logic right shift ) FOR AFT 2/ THEN NEXT ;
: ms ( n -- ) FOR AFT $1CB FOR NEXT THEN NEXT ;
: ud/mod ( ud1 n -- rem ud2 ) >R 0 R@ UM/MOD R> SWAP >R UM/MOD
R> ;
: bin ( -- ) 2 base ! ;

\  marker  is  easier  for  328eForth  with  only  one  vocabulary,
23mar11cht
: marker ( <new_name> -- )
    last @ dp @ cp @ context @
    create -2 cp +! , , , ,
    does r> 2* dup i@ context !
       2+ dup i@ cp !
       2+ dup i@ dp !
       2+ i@ last ! ;

flush
marker fence
```

```
\  Audio tone generator                          2010/01/08
\ Modified for 328eForth, 23mar11cht

\ Must have io-core.txt installed

chop-tone
marker chop-tone  \ a forget point

$44 value TCCR0A  \ Timer Counter Control Register A
\ mask  1100 0011
\ set   0100 0010  toggle output, generator mode [14-2, 14-8]

$45 value TCCR0B  \ Timer Control Control Register B
\ mask  0000 1111
\ set   0000 0xxx   WGM01 bit2, xxx is prescaler. [14-8]
\  0= counter off,  1= /1,  2=/8,  3=/64,  4=/256,  5=/1024

$47 value OCR0A  \ Output Comparison Register A
\ mask 1111 1111
\ set  <limit>   limit is 1..255 for counter. [14-9]

$29 value PortD     6 value Tone-out \ PortD bit 6
\ mask 0100 0000
\ set  0100 0000 or true  initialize pin as output

: setup-osc \ prescale limit  ---  limit 1..255, prescale 1..5
   PortD   Tone-out                PoBiOut \ setup output pin
   OCR0A   true      rot ( limit   ) RegTo     [ bin ]
   TCCR0A  11000011  01000010        RegTo    \ CTC mode
           00000101  min    0  max     \ form TCCR0B prescale
   TCCR0B  00001111 rot ( prescale ) RegTo ;   \ and tone on

: tone-off \  ---  end output tone setting prescale to zeros
   TCCR0B  00000111  false RegTo    ;  decimal

78 value Limit   4 value Prescale   \ 400 Hz tone parameters

: Hertz    \ frequency --- load Limit and Prescale
   $1200 $7A ( 8000000. ) rot ud/mod  \ total scale as
```

```
                                \rem double-quot
   dup            if ( >16 bits)  1024  5 else
   over $C000 and if ( >14 bits)   256  4 else
   over $F800 and if ( >10 bits)    64  3 else
   over $FF00 and if ( > 8 bits)     8  2 else   1  1
                     then then then then
   to Prescale  um/mod to Limit  drop drop
   ( two remainders ) ;

: tone-on   \ ---  begin tone from fixed presets
    Prescale  Limit  setup-osc ;

: note  \ duration ---  generate timed tone for duration msec.
    tone-on  ms  tone-off   ;

\ End of tone.txt
flush
```

```
\  Chronometer                   WFR 2011-01-27
\ Modified for 328eForth, 23mar11cht

\ must have io-core.txt installed

chop-chrono
marker chop-chrono  \ this forget point

$36 value TIFR1    \ has overlow bit
$43 value GTCCR    \ counter control register
$80 value TCCR1A   \ timer control register, no outputs
$81 value TCCR1B   \ prescaler factor
$84 value TCNT1lo  \ counter low 8 bits
$85 value TCNT1hi  \ counter high 8 bits

0  value  prescale  \ 0= stop; 1..5 is prescale setup

bin

: chrono-hack  \  --- count scale overflow
\ read continuing count
  TCNT1lo  true      RegFrom      \ lo byte
  TCNT1hi  true      RegFrom      \ hi byte
  $8 lshift or                    \ form count into 16 bits
  prescale                        \ include in output
  TIFR1    00000001  RegFrom ;    \  overflow bit

: chrono-stop  \  --- count scale overflow
\ stop chronometer returning its values
  false  TCCR1B c!  \ stop counter
                    \ via timer control register
  chrono-hack  ;    \ read chronometer values

: chrono-start  \  prescale ---
\ initialize and start chronometer using Timer 1
  dup 101 > abort" Prescale too high"  to prescale
  GTCCR   10000001  true  RegTo  \ halt counter,
                                 \ clear prescale
  TCCR1A  11110011  false    RegTo  \ no outputs,
```

```
                                   \ normal mode
  TCCR1B  11011111  prescale RegTo  \ set prescaler
   false  TCNT1hi    c!      \ must write directly,
                             \ clear counter hi
   false  TCNT1lo    c!      \ clear counter lo
  TIFR1   00000001  true     RegTo  \ clear overflow bit
  GTCCR   10000000  false    RegTo  \ start prescaler and
                                    \ counter
  ;

decimal

: chrono-norm  \ count scale overflow
              \ --- usec_double overflow
          \ normalize into count and microsecond multiplier
              \ for 1 & 2 truncated not rounded up.
 >r >r r@   1 = if  4 rshift 1  else \ 1 usec ..  4.095 msec
    r@   2 = if  1 rshift 1  else  \  1 usec .. 32.767 msec
    r@   3 = if           4  else  \  4 usec ..  0.262 sec
    r@   4 = if          16  else  \ 16 usec ..  1.048 sec
                         64        \ 64 usec ..  4.194 sec
        then then then then
  um*  r> drop r> ;  \ leave microseconds as a double number

: 1000/mod    \ double --- rem double/1000
   1000 ud/mod ;

: nnn ( n -- ) <# # # # #> TYPE ;
: nnn, ( n -- ) nnn ." ," ;
: n,n,n ( d -- )
 1000/mod 1000/mod DROP
 ?DUP IF . ." ," nnn, nnn ELSE
 ?DUP IF . ." ," nnn ELSE . THEN THEN ;

: chrono-report  \ count scale overflow ---
\  from chronometer reading display time,
\ observing the scale
   chrono-norm   abort" counter overflow"
   n,n,n ."  usec" ;
```

```
: chrono-count  \ count scale overflow ---
\ from chronometer reading,
\ report elapsed processor clock counts
\   with 484 count bias removed.
   abort" counter overflow"   >r  \ save scale
   r@ 1 = if  1 else  r@ 2 = if 8   else
     r@ 3 = if 64 else  r@ 4 = if 256
   else 1024 then then then then
   r> drop   um*  22976 0 d- ( remove overhead cycles )
   n,n,n  ."  clock counts" ;

\ Usage is:   3 chrono-start . . . chrono-stop chrono-report
\ Null time is 484 clock cycles or 30.25 usec.
\ This is the time for chrono-start exit and do-colon of
chrono-stop.
\ A test of 20 ms report gives  19.941 msec.
\         1000 ms report gives 995.136 msec.
\         4000 ms report gives   3.980 sec.
\ Adjusting for fixed offset time is .9955 of true time.

\ Read machine cycles: 1 chrono-start . . . chrono-stop chrono-
count

\ end of chronometer.txt
flush
```

```
\ DUMP utility to print memory                WFR 2011-01-03
\ Begin by specifying target memory: flash, ram, eeprom
\ Call dump with starting address and byte count

\ dump                    WFR 2011-01-27
\ Modified for 328eForth, 23mar11cht

marker chop-dump

decimal

1 value target  ( 0=flash, 1=ram)

: flash 0 to target ;

: ram   1 to target ;

: smartC@   ( addr --- cell-contents )
     target if C@ else iC@ then ;

: ?legal ( char --- printable_char from low 8 bits )
 255 and   32 over > over 127 > or   if drop $2E ( . ) then ;

: .location ( --- print memory bank being accessed)
   target if ."  ram " else ."  flash " then ;

: .alpha ( addr count --- print 8 cells or 16 bytes
          as ascii characters)
   for aft dup smartC@ ?legal emit 1+ then next drop ;

: .memory ( addr count --- flash prints cells; r/r prints
          bytes)
   for aft dup smartC@ 3 u.r 1+ then next drop ;

: dump ( addr count ---  form: 1234 xx xx xx xx xx abcdefg)
   .location cr   base @ >r   hex  16 /
   for aft dup 5 u.r dup 16 .memory dup 16 .alpha cr
   16 + then next drop r> base !  ;

\ end of dump utility
Flush
```

```
FLASHER.txt to Demo LED control             WFR 2011-01-27

( must have io-core.txt installed )

chop-flasher

marker chop-flasher  ( a forget point)

$23 value PortB  $26 value PortC  $29 value PortD
  5 value LED

: 1-cycle  ( ms_delay ---   flash LED on then off )
    PortB LED PoBiHi   dup ms   PortB LED PoBiLo   ms ;

: many  ( on_time flashes ---  produce controlled LED flashes)
    PortB LED PoBiOut ( set LED pin as output)
    for aft  dup 1-cycle then next drop ;

( use 'many' leading with on-time and # of flashes )

( end of flasher.txt )
flush
```

9 17 Lessons

```
( Example 1.       The Universal Greeting )

DECIMAL

: HELLO CR ." Hello, world!" ;
```

```
( Example 2.       The Big F )

: bar   CR ." *****" ;
: post  CR ." *    " ;
: F     bar post bar post post post ;

( Type 'F' and a return on your keyboard, )
( and you will see a large
F character displayed on the screen )
```

```
( Example 3.       FIG, Forth Interest Group )

: center CR ."   *  " ;
: sides  CR ." *   *" ;
: triad1 CR ." * * *" ;
: triad2 CR ." **  *" ;
: triad3 CR ." *  **" ;
: triad4 CR ."  *** " ;
: quart  CR ." ** **" ;
: right  CR ." * ***" ;
: bigT  bar center center center center center center ;
: bigI  center center center center center center center ;
: bigN  sides triad2 triad2 triad1 triad3 triad2 sides ;
: bigG  triad4 sides post right triad1 sides triad4 ;
: FIG  F bigI bigG ;
```

```
( Example 4.          Repeated Patterns )

FOR       [ index -- ]            Set up loop given the index.
NEXT      [ -- ]          Decrement index by 1.  If index<0, exit.
                             If index=limit, exit loop; otherwise
                                  Otherwise repeat after FOR.
R@        [ -- index ]           Return the current loop index. )


VARIABLE WIDTH                   ( number of asterisks to print )

: ASTERISKS ( -- , print n asterisks on the screen, n=width )
        WIDTH @                  ( limit=width, initial index=0 )
        FOR ." *"                ( print one asterisk at a time )
        NEXT                     ( repeat n times )
        ;

: RECTANGLE ( height width -- , print a rectangle of asterisks )
        WIDTH !                  ( initialize width to be printed
)
        FOR     CR
                ASTERISKS        ( print a line of asterisks )
        NEXT
        ;

: PARALLELOGRAM ( height width -- )
        WIDTH !
        FOR     CR R@ SPACES     ( shift the lines to the right )
                ASTERISKS        ( print one line )
        NEXT
        ;

: TRIANGLE ( width -- , print a triangle area with asterisks )
        FOR     CR
                R@ WIDTH !       ( increase width every line )
                ASTERISKS        ( print one line )
        NEXT
        ;
```

```
( Try the following instructions:

        3 10 RECTANGLE
        5 18 PARALLELOGRAM
        12 TRIANGLE  )
```

(Example 5. The Theory That Jack Built)

```
( This example shows you how to build a hiararchical structure
in Forth)

DECIMAL

: the           ." the " ;
: that          CR ." That " ;
: this          CR ." This is " the ;
: jack          ." Jack Builds" ;
: summary       ." Summary" ;
: flaw          ." Flaw" ;
: mummery       ." Mummery" ;
: k             ." Constant K" ;
: haze          ." Krudite Verbal Haze" ;
: phrase        ." Turn of a Plausible Phrase" ;
: bluff         ." Chaotic Confusion and Bluff" ;
: stuff         ." Cybernatics and Stuff" ;
: theory        ." Theory " jack ;
: button        ." Button to Start the Machine" ;
: child         ." Space Child with Brow Serene" ;
: cybernatics   ." Cybernatics and Stuff" ;

: hiding        CR ." Hiding " the flaw ;
: lay           that ." Lay in " the theory ;
: based         CR ." Based on " the mummery ;
: saved         that ." Saved " the summary ;
: cloak         CR ." Cloaking " k ;
: thick         IF that ELSE CR ." And " THEN
                ." Thickened " the haze ;
```

```
: hung          that ." Hung on " the phrase ;
: cover         IF that ." Covered "
                ELSE CR ." To Cover "
                THEN bluff ;
: make          CR ." To Make with " the cybernatics ;
: pushed        CR ." Who Pushed " button ;
: without       CR ." Without Confusion, Exposing the Bluff" ;

: rest                          ( pause for user interaction )
        ." . "                           ( print a period )
        10 SPACES                   ( followed by 10 spaces )
        KEY                       ( wait the user to press a key )
        DROP CR CR CR ;

(
KEY     [ -- char ]       Wait for a keystroke, and return the
                               ASCII code of the key pressed.
DROP    [ n -- ]               Discard the number.
SPACE   [ -- ]                 Display a blank.
SPACES  [ n -- ]               Display n blanks.
IF      [ f -- ]             If the flag is 0, skip the following
                          instructions up to ELSE or THEN.  If
                          flag is not 0, execute the following
                           instructions up to ELSE and skip to
                               THEN.
ELSE    [ -- ]                 Skip the following instructions
                               up to THEN.
THEN    [ -- ]               Terminate an IF-ELSE-THEN structure
                               or an IF-THEN structure.
)

: cloaked cloak saved based hiding lay rest ;

: THEORY
        CR this theory rest
        this flaw lay rest
        this mummery hiding lay rest
        this summary based hiding lay rest
        this k saved based hiding lay rest
```

```
        this haze cloaked
        this bluff hung 1 thick cloaked
        this stuff 1 cover hung 0 thick cloaked
        this button make 0 cover hung 0 thick cloaked
        this child pushed
                CR ." That Made with " cybernatics without hung
                CR ." And, Shredding " the haze cloak
                CR ." Wrecked " the summary based hiding
                CR ." And Demolished " the theory rest
        ;

( Type THEORY to start)
```

(Example 6.   Help)

```
( How to use Forth interpreter to carry on a dialog )

: question
        CR CR ." Any more problems you want to solve?"
        CR ." What kind ( sex, job, money, health ) ?"
        CR
        ;

: help  CR
        CR ." Hello!  My name is Creating Computer."
        CR ." Hi there!"
        CR ." Are you enjoying yourself here?"
        KEY 32 OR 89 =
        CR
        IF      CR ." I am glad to hear that."
        ELSE    CR ." I am sorry about that."
                CR ." maybe we can brighten your visit a bit."
        THEN
        CR ." Say!"
        CR ." I can solved all kinds of problems except those
dealing"
        CR ." with Greece. "
        question
```

```
        ;

: sex   CR CR ." Is your problem TOO MUCH or TOO LITTLE?"
        CR
        ;

: too  ;                        ( noop for syntax smoothness )

: much  CR CR ." You call that a problem?!!  I SHOULD have that
problem."
        CR ." If it reall y bothers you, take a cold shower."
        question
        ;

: little
        CR CR ." Why are you here!"
        CR ." You should be in Tokyo or New York of Amsterdam
or"
        CR ." some place with some action."
        question
        ;

: health
        CR CR ." My advise to you is:"
        CR ."      1. Take two tablets of aspirin."
        CR ."      2. Drink plenty of fluids."
        CR ."      3. Go to bed (along) ."
        question
        ;

: job   CR CR ." I can sympathize with you."
        CR ." I have to work very long every day with no pay."
        CR ." My advise to you, is to open a rental computer
store."
        question
        ;

: money
        CR CR ." Sorry!  I am broke too."
```

```
        CR ." Why don't you sell encyclopedias of marry"
        CR ." someone rich or stop eating, so you won't "
        CR ." need so much money?"
        question
        ;

: HELP help ;
: H help ;
: h help ;

( Type 'help' to start )
```

(Example 7. Money Exchange)

The first example we will use to demonstrate how numbers are used in Forth is a money exchange program, which converts money represented in different currencies. Let's start with the following currency exchange table:

```
        33.55 NT        1 Dollar
        7.73 HK         1 Dollar
        9.47 RMB        1 Dollar
        1 Ounce Gold    285 Dollars
        1 Ounce Silver  4.95 Dollars )

DECIMAL

: NT    ( nNT -- $ )    100 3355 */  ;
: $NT   ( $ -- nNT )    3355 100 */  ;
: RMB   ( nRMB -- $ )   100 947 */  ;
: $RMB  ( $ -- nJmp )   947 100 */  ;
: HK    ( nHK -- $ )    100 773 */  ;
: $HK   ( $ -- $ )      773 100 */  ;
: GOLD  ( nOunce -- $ ) 285 *  ;
: $GOLD ( $ -- nOunce ) 285 /  ;
: SILVER ( nOunce -- $ ) 495 100 */  ;
: $SILVER ( $ -- nOunce ) 100 495 */  ;
```

```
: OUNCE ( n -- n, a word to improve syntax )   ;
: DOLLARS ( n -- )        . ;

( With this set of money exchange words, we can do some tests:

        5 ounce gold .
        10 ounce silver .
        100 $NT .
        20 $RMB .

If you have many different currency bills in your wallet, you
can add then all up in dollars:

        1000 NT 500 HK + .S
        320 RMB + .S
        DOLLARS ( print out total worth in dollars )
```

(Example 8. Temperature Conversion

Converting temperature readings between Celcius and Farenheit is also an interesting problem. The difference between temperature
conversion and money exchange is that the two temperature scales have an offset besides the scaling factor.)

```
: F>C ( nFarenheit -- nCelcius )
        32 -
        10 18 */
        ;

: C>F ( nCelcius -- nFarenheit )
        18 10 */
        32 +
        ;

( Try these commands
```

```
90 F>C .        shows the temperature in a hot summer day and
0 C>F .         shows the temperature in a cold winter night.

In the above examples, we use the following Forth arithmatic
operators:

+      [ n1 n2 -- n1+n2 ]  Add n1 and n2 and leave sum on stack.
-      [ n1 n2 -- n1-n2 ] Subtract n2 from n1 and leave differrence
                                   on stack.
*      [ n1 n2 -- n1*n2 ]      Multiply n1 and n2 and leave product
                                   on stack.
/     [ n1 n2 -- n1/n2 ]     Divide n1 by n2 and leave quotient on
                                   stack.
*/  [ n1 n2 n3 -- n1*n2/n3] Multiply n1 and n2, divide the product
                             by n3 and leave quotient on the stack.
.S    [ ... -- ... ]          Show the topmost 4 numbers on stack.
)
```

(Example 9. Weather Reporting.)

```
: WEATHER ( nFarenheit -- )
        DUP     55 <
        IF      ." Too cold!" DROP
        ELSE    85 <
                IF      ." About right."
                ELSE    ." Too hot!"
                THEN
        THEN
        ;

( You can type the following instructions and get some responses
from the computer:

        90 WEATHER Too hot!
        70 WEATHER About right.
        32 WEATHER Too cold.
)
```

(Example 10. Print the multiplication table)

```
: ONEROW ( nRow -- )
       CR
       DUP 3 .R 3 SPACES
       1 11
       FOR     2DUP *
               4 .R
               1 +
       NEXT
       DROP ;

: MULTIPLY ( -- )
       CR CR 6 SPACES
       1 11
       FOR     DUP 4 .R 1 +
       NEXT DROP
       1 11
       FOR     DUP ONEROW 1 +
       NEXT DROP
       ;

( Type MULTIPLY to print the multiplication table )
```

(Example 11. Calendars)

```
( Print weekly calendars for any month in any year. )
DECIMAL

VARIABLE JULIAN               ( 0 is 1/1/1950, good until 2050 )
VARIABLE LEAP                ( 1 for a leap year, 0 otherwise. )
( 1461 CONSTANT 4YEARS            ( number of days in 4 years )

: YEAR ( YEAR --, compute Julian date and leap year )
       DUP
```

```
        1949 - 1461 4 */MOD             ( days since 1/1/1949 )
        365 - JULIAN !                  ( 0 for 1/1/1950 )
        3 =                        ( modulus 3 for a leap year )
        IF 1 ELSE 0 THEN                ( leap year )
        LEAP !
        DUP 2000 =                 ( 2000 is not a leap year )
        IF 0 LEAP ! THEN
        2001 <                       ( correction due to 2000 )
        IF ELSE -1 JULIAN +! THEN
        ;

: FIRST ( MONTH - 1ST, 1st of a month from Jan. 1 )
        DUP 1 =
        IF DROP 0 EXIT THEN             ( 0 for Jan. 1 )
        DUP 2 =
        IF DROP 31 EXIT THEN            ( 31 for Feb. 1 )
        DUP 3 =
        IF DROP 59 LEAP @ + EXIT THEN   ( 59/60 for Mar. 1 )
        4 - 30624 1000 */
        90 + LEAP @ +                   ( Apr. 1 to Dec. 1 )
        ;

: STARS 60 FOR 42 EMIT NEXT ;           ( form the boarder )

: HEADER ( -- )                         ( print title bar )
        CR STARS CR
        ."      SUN    MON    TUE    WED    THU    FRI    SAT"
        CR STARS CR                     ( print weekdays )
        ;
: BLANKS ( MONTH -- )          ( skip days not in this month )
        FIRST JULIAN @ +       ( Julian date of 1st of month )
        7 MOD 8 * SPACES ;     ( skip colums if not Sunday   )

: DAYS ( MONTH -- )                ( print days in a month )
        DUP FIRST                  ( days of 1st this month )
        SWAP 1 + FIRST             ( days of 1st next month )
        OVER - 1 -                 ( loop to print the days )
        1 SWAP                     ( first day count -- )
        FOR  2DUP + 1 -
```

```
                JULIAN @ + 7 MOD      ( which day in the week? )
                IF ELSE CR THEN     ( start a new line if Sunday )
                DUP  8 U.R         ( print day in 8 column field )
   1999       +
        NEXT
        2DROP ;                ( discard 1st day in this month )

: MONTH ( N -- )               ( print a month calendar )
        HEADER DUP BLANKS                ( print header )
        DAYS CR STARS CR ;               ( print days   )

: JANUARY       YEAR 1 MONTH ;
: FEBRUARY      YEAR 2 MONTH ;
: MARCH         YEAR 3 MONTH ;
: APRIL         YEAR 4 MONTH ;
: MAY           YEAR 5 MONTH ;
: JUNE          YEAR 6 MONTH ;
: JULY          YEAR 7 MONTH ;
: AUGUST        YEAR 8 MONTH ;
: SEPTEMBER     YEAR 9 MONTH ;
: OCTOBER       YEAR 10 MONTH ;
: NOVEMBER      YEAR 11 MONTH ;
: DECEMBER      YEAR 12 MONTH ;

( To print the calender of April 1999, type:
        1999 APRIL
)
```

(Example 12.   Sines and Cosines)

Sines and cosines of angles are among the most often encountered transdential functions, useful in drawing circles and many other different applications. They are usually computed using floating numbers for accuracy and dynamic range. However, for graphics applications in digital systems, single integers in the range from
-32768 to 32767 are sufficient for most purposes. We shall

study the computation of sines and cosines using the single integers.

The value of sine or cosine of an angle lies between -1.0 and +1.0.

We choose to use the integer 10000 in decimal to represent 1.0 in the computation so that the sines and cosines can be represented
with enough precision for most applications. Pi is therefore 31416, and 90 degree angle is represented by 15708. Angles are first reduced in to the range from -90 to +90 degrees, and then converted to radians in the ranges from -15708 to +15708. From the radians we compute the values of sine and cosine.

The sines and cosines thus computed are accurate to 1 part in 10000. This algorithm was first published by John Bumgarner in Forth Dimensions, Volume IV, No. 1, p. 7.

```
31415 CONSTANT PI
10000 CONSTANT 10K )
VARIABLE XS                      ( square of scaled angle )

: KN ( n1 n2 -- n3, n3=10000-n1*x*x/n2 where x is the angle )
        XS @ SWAP /                  ( x*x/n2 )
        10000 */ NEGATE                ( -n1*x*x/n2 )
        10000 +                        ( 10000-n1*x*x/n2 )
        ;

: (SIN) ( x -- sine*10K, x in radian*10K )
        DUP DUP 10000 */               ( x*x scaled by 10K )
        XS !                         ( save it in XS )
        10000 72 KN                    ( last term )
        42 KN 20 KN 6 KN             ( terms 3, 2, and 1 )
        10000 */                       ( times x )
        ;

: (COS) ( x -- cosine*10K, x in radian*10K )
        DUP 10000 */ XS !          ( compute and save x*x )
```

```
        10000 56 KN 30 KN 12 KN 2 KN          ( serial expansion )
        ;

: SIN ( degree -- sine*10K )
        31415 180 */                         ( convert to radian )
        (SIN)                               ( compute sine )
        ;

: COS ( degree -- cosine*10K )
        31415 180 */
        (COS)
        ;


( To test the routines, type:

        90 SIN .                         9999
        45 SIN .                         7070
        30 SIN .                         5000
         0 SIN .                            0
        90 COS .                            0
        45 COS .                         7071
         0 COS .                         10000 )
```

(Example 13. Square Root)

There are many ways to take the square root of an integer. The special routine here was first discovered by Wil Baden. Wil used this routine as a programming challenge while attending a FORML Conference in Taiwan, 1984.

This algorithm is based on the fact that the square of n+1 is equal
to the sum of the square of n plus 2n+1. You start with an 0 on
the stack and add to it 1, 3, 5, 7, etc., until the sum is greater

than the integer you wished to take the root. That number when you stopped is the square root.
)

```
: SQRT ( n -- root )
        65025 OVER U<              ( largest square it can handle)
        IF DROP 255 EXIT THEN          ( safety exit )
        >R                             ( save sqaure )
        1 1                           ( initial square and root )
        BEGIN                           ( set n1 as the limit )
                OVER R@ U<                ( next square )
        WHILE
                DUP CELLS 1 +             ( n*n+2n+1 )
                ROT + SWAP
                1 +                       ( n+1 )
        REPEAT
        SWAP DROP
        R> DROP
        ;
```

(Example 14.   Radix for Number Conversions)

```
DECIMAL

( : DECIMAL       10 BASE ! ; )
( : HEX           16 BASE ! ; )
: OCTAL         8 BASE !  ;
: BINARY        2 BASE !  ;

( Try converting numbers among different radices:

        DECIMAL 12345 HEX U.
        HEX ABCD DECIMAL U.
        DECIMAL 100 BINARY U.
        BINARY 101010101010 DECIMAL U.
```

Real programmers impress on novices by carrying a HP calculator which can convert numbers between decimal and hexadecimal. A Forth computer has this calculator built in, besides other functions.
)

(Example 15. ASCII Character Table)

```
: CHARACTER ( n -- )
        DUP EMIT HEX DUP 3 .R
        OCTAL DUP 4 .R
        DECIMAL 3 .R
        2 SPACES
        ;

: LINE ( n -- )
        CR
        5 FOR   DUP CHARACTER
                16 +
        NEXT
        DROP ;

: TABLE ( -- )
        32
        15 FOR  DUP LINE
                1 +
        NEXT
        DROP ;
```

```
( Example 16.  Random Numbers

Random  numbers  are  often  used  in  computer  simulations  and
computer
games.   This  random  number  generator  was  published  in  Leo
Brodie's
'Starting Forth'.
)

VARIABLE RND                               ( seed )
HERE RND !                                 ( initialize seed )

: RANDOM ( -- n, a random number within 0 to 65536 )
        RND @ 31421 *                      ( RND*31421 )
        6927 +                         ( RND*31421+6926, mod 65536)
        DUP RND !                          ( refresh he seed )
        ;

: CHOOSE ( n1 -- n2, a random number within 0 to n1 )
        RANDOM UM*                 ( n1*random to a double product)
        SWAP DROP                          ( discard lower part )
        ;                              ( in fact divide by 65536 )

( To test the routine, type

        100 CHOOSE .
        100 CHOOSE .
        100 CHOOSE .

and varify that the results are randomly distributed betweem 0
and 99 . )
```

```
( Example 17.       Guess a Number )

: GetNumber ( -- n )
        BEGIN
                CR ." Enter a Number: " ( show message )
                QUERY BL WORD NUMBER?   ( get a string )
        UNTIL                       ( repeat until a valid number )
        ;

( With this utility instruction, we can write a game 'Guess a
Number.' )

: InitialNumber ( -- n , set up a number for the player to guess
)
        CR CR CR ." What limit do you want?"
        GetNumber          ( ask the user to enter a number )
        CR ." I have a number between 0 and " DUP .
        CR ." Now you try to guess what it is."
        CR
        CHOOSE                       ( choose a random number )
        ;                            ( between 0 and limit )

: Check ( n1 -- , allow player to guess, exit when the guess is
correct )
        BEGIN   CR ." Please enter your guess."
                GetNumber
                2DUP =                       ( equal? )
                IF      2DROP               ( discard both numbers )
                        CR ." Correct!!!"
                        EXIT
                THEN
                OVER <
                IF      CR ." Too low."
                ELSE    CR ." Too high!"
                THEN    CR
        0 UNTIL                              ( always repeat )
        ;

: Greet ( -- )
```

```
        CR CR CR ." GUESS A NUMBER"
        CR ." This is a number guessing game.  I'll think"
        CR ." of a number between 0 and any limit you want."
        CR ." (It should be smaller than 32000.)"
        CR ." Then you have to guess what it is."
        ;

: GUESS ( -- , the game )
        Greet
        BEGIN   InitialNumber                 ( set initial number)
                Check                         ( let player guess )
                CR CR ." Do you want to play again? (Y/N) "
                KEY                                 ( get one key )
                32 OR 110 =                         ( exit if it is
N or n )
        UNTIL
        CR CR ." Thank you.  Have a good day."  ( sign off )
        CR
        ;


( Type 'GUESS' will initialize the game and the computer will
entertain
a user for a while.  Note the use of the indefinite loop
structure:

        BEGIN <repeat-clause> [ f ] UNTIL

You can jump out of the infinite loop by the instruction EXIT,
which
skips all the instructions in a Forth definition up to ';', which
terminates this definition and continues to the next definition.
)
```

10 My Electronic Bookshelf

A couple of years ago, I closed my website www.offete.com and stopped distributing my publications on-line. Nevertheless, these publications still exist on my electronic bookshelf. If you need any of them, please send me a request at chenhting@yahoo.com.tw, I will sent it in a return email, and also bill you by a PayPal invoice. I know, we are in the 21st century now. You cannot do anything without a website. But, at least I got rid of lots of paper, and the snail mail.

Juergen Pintaske twisted my arm to get *Footsteps in an Empty Valley* updated from a printed copy, which was edited on an old word processor TMaker on a CP/M machine and printed with a Diablo daisy wheel printer. Files got lost with the CP/M machine. I had to scan all the pages and used OCR to recover the text. The hardest part was Chuck Moore's source code of cmForth, which he printed on an Epson dot matrix printer with a worn ribbon. Lots of the dots disappeared through copying processes. I tried my best to bring back the code, but couldn't be entirely sure. I hope nobody will use the code for any purpose other than reading.

Well. Let me know if you have any question.

Chen-Hanson Ting,
San Mateo, California
February, 2017

PDF Books

After I learnt a Forth system, I always tried to document it so I could teach other people how to use it. So I wrote about polyForth, figForth, F83, F-PC, and cmForth. When Win32Forth came along, I gave up, because it was too large and too complicated. I then focused on developing eForth for microcontrollers. After retirement, I cleaned out the books off my shelves. People still asked for them, so I converted some to pdf files. Here is the list of available titles:

4001 Footsteps in an Empty Valley, 4th Ed., $15
Description of the first Forth chip NC4000 from Novix, and Chuck Moore's cmForth for it. cmForth was the simplest and most compact specification of a real Forth system

for a real Forth computer. It contains a complete Forth system with a target compiler, an optimizing assembler, and a serial disk driver. Required reading for all Forth programmers.

1010 Systems Guide to figForth, 3rd Ed., $15

The most authoritative treatise on how's and why's of the figForth Model developed by Bill Ragsdale. Internal structure of the figForth system. Very detailed discussions on the inner interpreters and the outer (text) interpreter of Forth.

1003 Inside F83, $15

Everything you want to know about the Perry-Laxen F83 system but afraid to ask. 288 packed pages divided into 4 parts: Tutorial on F83 system, Kernel, Utility, and Tools. It is based on 8086 F83 Version 2.1 for the IBM-PC, but useful as a reference manual for all other (8080 and 68000) F83 systems.

1008 F-PC Technical Reference Manual, $15

Narration on all words in the kernel and tools of F-PC, a practically useful Forth system for applications on PC. Functional description of the utilities and applications. Valuable guide to F-PC internals and assembly coding on segmented 80386 architecture.

1013 .eForth and Zen, 3rd Ed. $15

Complete description and exposition of the eForth Model: kernel, high level words, interpreters, compiler and utilities. Comparison of Forth and Zen, their similarities in simplicity and understanding. It is update based on 32-Bit 586 eForth v5.2 for Visual Studio Community 2015. It is in an assembly file as a C++ console project. It uses indirect thread model so that new colon words can be added to the .data segment. It is optimized with 71 code words and 110 colon words.

1015 Firmware Engineering Workshop, $15

A tutorial in 4 parts for building firmware for embedded systems, based on enhanced eForth. Hands-on experiments using CT100 Lab Board with 8051. 8086 eForth 2.02 and 8051 eForth 2.03 are included with the original eForth 1.01 Models for 8086 and 8051.

eForth Implementations

I had always looked for low-cost microcontroller kits to teach people Forth. Over the years, these kits were getting cheaper and more powerful, and I ported eForth to a lots of them. I had lots of fun with them, and I enjoyed seeing others having fun (and making useful products) as well. eForth captures the essence of Forth, as an universal programming language for small, embedded systems. These eForth implementations are distributed with source code and substantial documentation.

2152 ADuC ARM7 eForth, $25
eForth for ADuC7020 MicroConverters from Analog Devices. It is written in ARM7 assembler on a Keil IDE. It uses the ARM7 link register for threading, and is fully optimized to make the best use of ARM7 core and analog peripherals integrated in this true microcontroller.

2153 SAM7 ARM7 eForth, $25
eForth for AT91SAM7X256 microcontroller from Atmel. It is in ARM7 assembler on Keil uVision3 RealView IDE. It uses the DBGU serial port to interact with user. Olimex's SAM7-EX256 Board has a very interest color LCD module. This eForth has graphic primitives to drive the LCD display.

2154 cEF Version 1.0, $25
cEF is a Forth implementation based on eForth Model, and compiled by gcc compiler in Cygwin on a PC. The underlying Virtual Forth Machine has the standard 33 machine instructions defined in the original eForth Model. It is target to microprocessor without floating point coprocessor, and uses only integer arithmetic operations.

2155 cEF Version 2.0, $25
cEF is a Forth implementation based on eForth Model, and compiled by gcc compiler in Cygwin. The Virtual Forth Machine has 64 machine instructions. Multiplication and division are implemented using double arithmetic floating operations. It is highly optimized to take advantages of recent microprocessors with floating point coprocessors.

2157 eForth for STM8S,$25
STM8S is an 8 bit microcontroller from STMicroelectronics. ST is distributing a STM8S-Discovery Board for less than $10. It is an excellent kit to learn microcontroller programming. Now, a good Forth experimental kit is available for high school students.

2159 328eForth for Arduino Uno, $25

This is a very efficient implementation of eForth for ATmega328P microcontroller used on Arduino Uno Kit. It is using Subroutine Thread Model. It uses tools in NRWW memory to compile new words in main RWW flash memory. It allows you to build turnkey systems for commercial applications. It requires a flash programming tool.

2162 ceForth_328 for Arduino Uno, $25

This is an Arduino sketch which can be compiled and uploaded by Arduino IDE. The Forth Virtual Machine is coded in C, and the Forth dictionary is imported as a data array. The Forth dictionary can be extended into the RAM memory, so you can add new commands to this system. The dictionary is produced by a metacompiler running under F#. The source code of the metacompiler is included for you to enhance this system.

2164 430eForth for TI LaunchPad, $25

This is a Forth system for the MSP430G2553 microcontroller used on the LaunchPad from TI. It is a 16-bit Forth implementation to be assembler by the Code Composer Studio 5.2. It makes the best used of the 16 KB of flash memory, leaving about 10 KB for your applications.

2165 STM32eForth720 for STM32 F4 Discovery, $25

This eForth is for STM32F407 chip on STM32 F4 Discovery Kit from STMicroelectronics. This chip has 1 MB flash memory, 192 KB of RAM, and a ton of interesting IO devices. STM32 is no longer an ARM7 chip, but a THUMB2 chip. STMeForth720 is optimized for the new environment.

2166 430eForth v4.3 for TI LaunchPad, $25

This is a Forth system optimized for the MSP430G2553 microcontroller used on the LaunchPad from TI. It is changed from a subroutine threaded model to a direct threaded model, faster and more compact.

2167 8086 eForth Version 2.03, , $25

Enhanced 32-bit eForth for 80586 running under Visual Studio Community 2015. It is assembled by MASM buried under C++ as a console project. Now you can evaluate the eForth model conveniently in latest Windows environment.

2171 32-Bit 586eForth v.5.2 for Visual Studio, $25

It is a assembly file in a C++ console project on Visual Studio Community 2015. It requires library files supplied by Kip Irvine for Windows services. It uses indirect thread model so that new colon words can be added to the data segment. It is optimized with 71 code words and 110 colon words. Now you can test drive eForth on newer Windows PC.

2172 espForth for ESP866 Chip, $25
ESP8266 is a 32-bit microcontroller with integrated WiFi antenna and software drivers. Arduino IDE can compile and upload applications to it. espForth is an Arduino sketch which allows Forth commands to be sent to ESP8266 remotely as UDP packets. IoT for fun!

VHDL Forth Chip Designs

I had used VHDL to design Forth processors and tested them on FPGA's. They included a 16-bit processor eP16 and a 32-bit processor eP32. I ported eForth to these chips for design verification. In 2016, we ran a CPU Design Workshop in Silicon Valley Forth Interest Group, and I used designs of Intel 8080 and DEC PDP1 as exercises. It was interesting that eForth was used here as test benches, which were much more difficult to design than CPU themselves.

2163 eP16 in VHDL for LatticeXP2 Brevia Kit, $25
eP16 is a 16 bit microcontroller. It was implemented on LatticeXP2 Brevia Development Kit with LatticeXP2-5E FPGA. It included a CPU module, a UART module and a GPIO module. An eForth metacompiler producing eForth RAM image is included with all source code.

2158 eP32 in VHDL for LatticeXP2 Brevia Kit, $25
eP32 is a 32 bit microcontroller. It was implemented on LatticeXP2 Brevia Development Kit with LatticeXP2-5E FPGA. It includes a CPU module, a UART module and a GPIO module. An eForth metacompiler producing eForth RAM image. It is the best Forth engine design on the cheapest FPGA kit. All VHDL files and eForth files are included.

2169 80eForth202 for eP8080 Chip, $25
eP8080 was a CPU model used in SVFIG FPGA Design Workshop. It recreated an i8080 chip in FPGA. 80eForth202 was the Forth system embedded in VHDL for design verification and to help debugging the chip. The eForth RAM image was derived from 86eForth v2.2 and Z80eForth by Ken Chen, assembled with MASM.

2170 PDP1eForth for ePDP1 Chip, $25

ePDP1 was another CPU model used in SVFIG FPGA Design Workshop. It recreated a PDP1 chip in FPGA. PDP1eForth was the Forth system embedded in VHDL for design verification and to help debugging the chip. It was derived from eP16, and used a metacompiler in F# to create eForth dictionary to initialize RAM memory.

This closes the last part of this eBook.

We do appreciate feedback, please to the publisher.
Any corrections to be made - for example.
Thank you very much in advance.
Please to epldfpga@aol.com.

####

Dr. Chen-Hanson Ting

Introduction:

Retired chemist-turned-engineer

For how long have you been interested in Forth: 32 years

Biography:

PhD in chemistry, University of Chicago, 1965.
Professor of chemistry in Taiwan until 1975.
Firmware engineer in Silicon Valley until retirement in 2000.
Still actively composing Forth Haikus.

Custodian of the eForth systems since 1990,
still maintaining eForth systems for Arduino,
MSP430, and various ARM microcontrollers.

Author of eP8, eP16, eP24, and eP32 microcontrollers in VHDL,
which were implemented on several FPGA chips.

Offete Enterprises, started in 1975, and is now formally closed.

However, Dr. Ting can still be contacted
through email chenhting@yahoo.com.tw
www.forth.org/whoswho.html#chting)
https://sites.google.com/offete23.com/eforth/home

ExMark Exeter 27 October 2018

www.ingramcontent.com/pod-product-compliance
Lightning Source LLC
Chambersburg PA
CBHW051049050326
40690CB00006B/654
9781726868471